MW01177930

VOICES MATTER

Jane-Finch Residents Speak Out

Angelo Furlan, Editor

JFOTM Books
Toronto, Ontario
Canada

ii

Jane-Finch On The Move

iv

Copyright © 2014 JFOTM Books

Library and Archives Canada Cataloguing in Publication

Voices matter: Jane-Finch residents speak out / Angelo Furlan, editor.

ISBN 978-0-9921492-0-8

1. Inner cities--Ontario--Toronto. 2. Community life--Ontario--Toronto. 3. Jane-Finch (Toronto, Ont.)--Social conditions.
I. Furlan, Angelo, 1958-, editor

HN110.T6V65 2014   307.7609713'541
C2014-903734-1

JFOTM Books
56 Clayhall Crescent
Toronto, Ontario, Canada
M3J 1W6

www.jfotm.com

Printed in U.S.A.

Dedications

To my parents, Efrem and Vannina, for their never ending support. And to everyone who's ever dared to dream - don't give up! Angelo

To the past, the present, and the future; to my mother (R.I.P.), my children, and the young lives this book will be affecting and enlightening. Celena

To my mother, Safy. Mom, you are my hero and inspiration, without you I would not be half the person I am. "I'll love you forever, I'll like you for always, As long as I'm living my Mommy you'll be." Mohamed

To my wonderful mother, and all the strong single mothers in the world. Mahmoud

To Jane-Finch On The Move: I have no idea where this group is going, I only know that I am better off knowing all these members than if I had not joined. We have become a family. Thank you, Jane-Finch On The Move. Maize

To my mother, Rose, who is my foundation. She is the woman I most want to be like. A woman who knows what she wants, and learns how to do what she wants, no matter how many obstacles are in her way. Marcia

To my wonderful sons who give meaning and purpose to my life. I am so proud to have them. Amina (Safy)

To the improvement in the lives of the underprivileged and those with disabilities, who share our world and our neighbourhood. Walter

To my children Jewelle and Joshua, I would like to let you know that your circumstances do not dictate your future, regardless of how terrible they may be. As long as you have a passion to succeed, and work towards that passion, you will achieve your goals. Chavenne

Here's to my partner in life! Let's work towards a bright future for our son and the future of the children. "A wise person will always find a way." Sandy

I want to thank God for giving me the opportunities to see the before and after of how the system operates living in and outside of Jane and Finch. Also thanking my family, children, husband and close friends for supporting me in all aspects of Life. Alicia

Thank God that I have the chance to join groups like Jane-Finch On The Move and learn about issues and concerns in our community. Wesley

To my husband and son: thanks for their love and patience. I owe it all to them. Mavis

Table of Contents

Introduction

It was a few years ago that I found myself walking along the east side of Jane Street, just north of the Driftwood Community Centre (4401 Jane Street). The mid morning sky was blue, the sun shined bright, and there was no one else in sight. The silence was a bit surprising, given that I was only minutes north of the Jane-Finch intersection and standing across the street from three large apartment buildings.

"Do you want an apple, sir?"

The young voice caught me by surprise. I whirled around, but as I said, there was no one else in sight. My reaction made the mystery voice chuckle, and that's when my ears placed him. I didn't realize I had walked by a tree; in fact, I had walked by a line of trees (what can I say? I'm not a particularly observant person). So I looked up.

There was a black child sitting up in the tree. With the passing of time, I don't recall the exact details of the conversation beyond that initial greeting. I do remember that my mystery man was extremely well-mannered for his age and in good humour. The tree was full of apples, and I soon learned that it was not the only one. The child attended Brookview Middle School, and he and some classmates were sent out to harvest the crop, as it were. I turned down the offer, largely because I had a sudden vision of my new friend getting in trouble because he came in short one apple.

I certainly do remember that when we finished talking, I had a big smile on my face. Apple trees near Jane and Finch - who knew? I didn't, and I've lived in the area since I was three years old.

Now, be honest. Was that the kind of story you expected to read in the opening chapter of a book about the Jane-Finch area?

Maybe you were expecting something like the following lead from a newspaper article written in 2008:

"Jane and Finch. What started as an urban planning dream quickly became a disaster and developed into a notorious neighbourhood where youth go to die or go prior to jail."[1]

Let's not sugar coat anything. The Jane-Finch neighbourhood does have issues. Some of these issues are the kind that come with any area that has a high population density. And a lot of people live in Jane-Finch. For example, there are three apartment buildings on the northeast corner of the Jane-Finch intersection, including one with 33 floors. These buildings, located at 5, 10, and 25 San Romanoway, have 892 units among them, and house around 4,400 people.[2]

While those three buildings are likely the largest in the area, they're certainly not the only ones. In fact, there are fourteen highrises along the four kilometre stretch of Jane Street from Steeles Avenue West to Sheppard Avenue West. These are just the buildings with a Jane Street address, as the San Romanoway buildings weren't included. There are even more highrises if one goes down roads such as Driftwood Avenue, Grandravine Drive, and Tobermory Drive. In the area north of Finch between Black Creek and Highway 400, "62.1 percent of dwellings are in buildings with five or more floors."[3]

Other issues come from the area's demographics - compared to Toronto overall, there are more racialized groups, more immigrants, more single parents, more lower income families, more unemployment, more community housing, and so on.

Take these issues and stir them together, and one might expect to find an area that is lawless and violent, an area that steadily cranks out lurid headlines, a notorious area "where youth go to die." Recent murder rates (2011) tell a slightly different tale. In the top ten most lethal neighbourhoods of Toronto, the closest we get to a Jane-Finch location is Downsview-Roding-CFB, and it came in at number nine.[4] None of the actual neighbourhoods that make up Jane-Finch were in the top ten.

This doesn't change the fact that Jane-Finch has issues. As I write this (summer 2013), the community is mourning the shooting death of a fifteen year old, the second such tragedy in six months. When fifteen year olds are being shot dead, all is definitely not well. However, it should be noted that there were only three murders in 2013. Perhaps there was a time where Jane-Finch stood out on its own when it came to senseless violence, but the sad reality is that Toronto now has many neighbourhoods with similar issues.[5] Yet, it is "Jane-Finch" that still resonates as a synonym for all that is wrong with the so-called inner city.

The purpose of this book is to go beyond the statistics, the headlines, and the generalizations. There are over fifty thousand people living in this neighbourhood, but it seems the only time any of them get heard is when there's a tragedy, or there's a story that reveals signs of hope in Jane-Finch; in other words, stories that perpetuate the image of Jane-Finch as a suburban wasteland. This book is an opportunity for various residents to speak freely about our lives and about what is important to us. This is a chance to be seen as something more than a statistic or a stereotype.

Most of the people interviewed for this book are members of Jane-Finch On The Move (JFOTM). The group was formed as a result of a community forum organized by various area organizations and agencies in March 2007. The first meeting took place on May 31 that year, and the group's name was chosen on July 17, 2007. The group has been meeting on a regular basis ever since. Initially, JFOTM meetings had support staff and agency representatives in attendance. Over time, the group evolved to where it is now an all volunteer group, made up of current and former residents of the area. The main criterion for membership is a passion for the Jane-Finch community. Eight of the members have been with the group since the first meeting back in May 2007, so there is a great deal of continuity within JFOTM.[6]

In order to represent the thoughts of group members, the material was mostly gathered through meetings with members in groups ranging in size from two persons up to eight. Some of these sessions were free-ranging, while others deliberately centred on topics that were of particular interest to members. Most of the sessions were recorded on digital devices and then transcribed and edited by JFOTM's Chair, who happens to be the same person writing this introduction. In a few cases, members borrowed a recording device and spoke to friends and other members of the community. Those recordings were also transcribed and appear in this book. Some members submitted written pieces.

During the interview and initial transcribing process, members decided they wanted to maintain their anonymity. In some cases, the editor changed minor details to ensure members' privacy would be protected. Otherwise, everything in this book comes directly from the mouths of residents, free to express their personal points of view. There was no attempt made to have everyone share a common viewpoint on any subject. Residents of Jane-Finch are individuals, each with their own experiences, values, and opinions.

The material was sorted by topic and placed into the appropriate chapter. Some members and residents discussed personal aspects of their lives in detail, and in those cases, they got a chapter titled "My Story." The chapter headings and brief description of each are in the Table of Contents.

Feel free to skip from section to section, even from paragraphs on the page. The book has been set up as a series of comments and conversations so it's more readily accessible. If you live in the Jane-Finch community, perhaps you'll see something that speaks to your own experiences. If you live outside the area, perhaps you'll gain a better

4

understanding for life in our community. We hope readers will find something that will inspire, illuminate, or perhaps even infuriate. A major purpose of this book is to start discussions and stimulate imaginations. It would be very satisfying to encourage fresh thinking about social issues. In every case, thank you for reading.

Angelo Furlan, Chair
Jane-Finch On The Move

Notes

[1] "Fear at the corner of guns 'n' drugs," *Toronto Sun*, 23 March 23 2008.

[2] "Turning a rundown highrise into a community hub," *Toronto Daily Star* 12 January 2011.

[3] Julie-Anne Boudreau, Roger Keil, Douglas Young. 2009. *Changing Toronto: Governing Urban Neoliberalism*. Toronto: University of Toronto Press.

[4] CBC News, "10 neighbourhoods for most per capita crime in 2011," http://www.cbc.ca/news/canada/toronto/story/2012/10/23/toronto-top-10-crime-neighbourhoods126.html; the neighbourhoods are ranked by murders per 10,000 residents. The closest Downsview-Roding-CFB comes to the Jane-Finch intersection is Jane Street, south of Sheppard Avenue West, which is two kilometres away. The neighbourhoods which form the Jane-Finch area are Black Creek and Glenfield-Jane Heights. For more information on the boundaries, visit here: http://www.toronto.ca/demographics/profiles_map_and_index.htm

[5] J. David Hulchanski discusses the substantial increase of low income areas within the City of Toronto in his report, "The Three Cities Within Toronto." At the time of writing, a digital copy could be found here: http://www.urbancentre.utoronto.ca/pdfs/curp/tnrn/Three-Cities-Within-Toronto-2010-Final.pdf

[6] To learn more about Jane-Finch On The Move, visit www.jfotm.com

First Impressions

People talk about their initial experiences with the Jane-Finch area.

I was living at Jane Street and Wilson Avenue, and I had my name on the waiting list for subsidized housing. I asked for anything along Jane because my mother lived at Jane and Falstaff Avenue and I wanted to be close to her. So approximately two years after I applied, I received a letter saying there was a property in the Jane-Finch area that I could view and if I liked it, I'd be able to accept the offer. That's pretty much how I came here. I remember when I told friends I was going to be moving here, they were saying, "Are you crazy? Do you have a death wish?"

It was interesting because at that time I was a single mother with two children and I was living in a one bedroom apartment. So if I was getting an opportunity to get a two bedroom at a cheaper rate, I would take my chances. I found within my first few months living here that the residents were more welcoming than what I was used to.

◆

It's been over seven years since I came to Jane and Finch. I used to come here before that for a lot of recreational stuff in the area. It was like a second home. I had heard a lot about Jane and Finch, actually.

Back in the day, you'd hear a lot of things about violence in the community. But one thing you notice is that there is a lot of heart and there is a lot of spirit here. The community works together when it's time to focus on progress. You have a lot of community support.

It took me some time to warm up to the area. That was because of the things you hear living outside the community and the image that's portrayed in the media - a lot of negative things that make it seem like an area that's not livable. Until you get here and you find it's quite the contrary. There's a lot of good things happening here and a lot of good movements happening here.

I came from Chalkfarm[1] which was a tight community, but we didn't have groups that organized around issues. Jane-Finch has great organizations. I didn't get involved in organizing until I came to Jane-Finch, and I was invited to join.

It's like a whole new world in itself. When you come into these organizations, you meet a lot of people, and you learn a lot about different cultures and even about what's going on around the world without being there.

That's what makes Jane-Finch special because there's so many different walks of life and people who do things together. It's a beautiful community. Coming into these organizations was a very good step because I started to feel a sense of fulfilment in being able to give back and play a role in making change, which was great.

I enjoy living in Jane-Finch. I feel there's still a lot that I would like to do in the community.

Looking from the outside, people see this as an unfriendly place, but when you're actually here, it's different. It's easy to see someone on the street and say hello. It's easy to sit amongst your peers and have a conversation. You see each other in the same circles, so eventually there's that sense of safety.

◆

The reason I came to Jane-Finch is that I moved into a building (215 Gosford Boulevard) where the rent was fairly cheap and it wasn't hard to get into and at that time, I had my daughter and my son.

The stereotype that there was about Jane-Finch having all the violence made me not want to move here, but I soon realized that a lot of the stereotypes were made up by the media, and made up by people trying to get money to do whatever. I noticed that a lot of people were trying to get money from funders by giving Jane-Finch a bad image. They would use this money to do some good and some bad.

Before I moved here, I was into organizations because I started a Teen Moms group with Black Creek[2] and it gave me that insight to want to go out there and help in any way, try to make a difference to teen mothers. I wanted to let people know that just because we were teen mothers, we weren't only wanting to be on welfare and not want to do anything with our lives.

I wanted these other ladies to know that this wasn't the end of the world - we could do things, we could participate in programs and try to improve our lives. When I moved to Gosford and realized the media image wasn't true, I said I could make a difference here. I could help other people have a different view. Then I moved out of Jane-Finch to somewhere else. I noticed that it wasn't the same. I felt like my work, what I wanted to do, was better off in Jane-Finch.

When you're outside Jane-Finch, people are more aloof, they feel like they're better than the people who are living in these areas. So I came back to Jane-Finch because I got housing in the Lanes (Yorkwoods

Village). I noticed that the image they had down there wasn't what people said it was. When I started talking to people, I noticed they didn't want to be that way, it's the media image, what outside people said, that's why they had to act it out, but they weren't really like that.

Once I was here, I started participating in various events, programs, meetings, and all that and I felt like there was a kind of family, a sense of belonging. Jane-Finch is so different from all the other areas I've been through. When everyone comes together, it's for something with good impact, to bring a positive image to Jane-Finch. When I go to these meetings, when I do these events, it's because I want the world to know that Jane-Finch is not how the media portrays it.

This is actually a place where you can live, where people get along, where you can learn about different cultures. That's the reason why I stay in Jane-Finch, that's the reason why I love Jane-Finch. If I could find and buy a big house in Jane-Finch, I would stay here.

◆

I moved into my house in 1967. It was a really good deal, I thought. Twenty-eight thousand, five hundred dollars with a thirty year mortgage at six and a half percent. The mortgage ran until 1993. The house was three years old. Streets like Hullmar Drive were not yet built. There was a farm house on the corner of Jane and Finch. The Jane-Finch Mall was being built at that time.

◆

I came to Jane-Finch in 1980. I got married in Egypt. I came here not knowing anybody, having no family and no friends. It was very hard for me the first time I came to Canada because I couldn't speak the main language. It took me a very long time to get in touch with other people that are of the same descent or share the same cultural background as me.

I did go to school here to get familiar with English mainly. Eventually I learned English which made it much easier for me to communicate with people. It took me a while to get used to Canada, with the bad weather and the open kissing in public. I'm not used to that, being from Egypt.

◆

I lived in Jane-Finch from when I was fifteen to just shy of eighteen. My mom was big on moving from place to place. I wasn't. A lot of my friends were still here, so I had to come back to be with them. I skipped school to be with my friends, and a lot of the Sunday school kids grew up here too. Basically, my friend base was still here, so we'd get together at the Jane-Finch Mall every Saturday and Sunday faithfully if I wasn't working. After school, on long weekends, I was always here. One of my friend's mother was really good friends with my mother, so that's why I know this area so well.

Then we moved to Finch and Islington Avenue, and still I'd travel along Finch to maintain friendships and such. Even though I had my own community, I never really knew anybody any place where I lived. I only knew people here in Jane-Finch.

I did a business course and I did my placement here at Jane/Finch Community and Family Centre (JFCFC),[3] and that's when I either reconnected with old friends or met new people, and got involved in programs here.

I was looking for a West African dance company for my daughter and ended up choosing one at the Driftwood Community Centre. That's where we were every Saturday for four or five years. It became a ritual every Saturday that we were in the area from morning until about six in the evening. So we're always here!

Then I would help my now in-laws with the store that they own in the Jane-Finch Mall. I would work there through the week, Saturdays and Sundays. For some reason, no matter where I go, I end up full-circle back in the Jane-Finch community.

My community work has always brought me back here as well, but I've never been active in my own community; that is, where I live now. I find it's more proactive here in Jane-Finch. I find there are many more things getting done here.

It's just this year (2013) that I've actually met some people in my area who are taking an interest, and found out about some programs that are going on. I've sat in on meetings where people notice I have some ideas. I have a lot of ideas and it's sad that I live in an area where you can't act on them. I'm not too happy about that.

◆

There aren't too many members sharing my nationality in this neighbourhood; actually, there aren't too many of us across Canada in general. There's about seventy thousand of us in this country. Coming from a single parent household, I always felt sad that I never had big family gatherings, no one to celebrate the big holidays like Christmas, Thanksgiving, and the others where you feed the kids and everyone gets excited. Instead, it was always just my mother and I. So not having a big family was something that always made me feel bad.

◆

I was born here. I got a diploma in Social Citizenship, and haven't found a job yet. My issue with Jane and Finch is that there is too much stereotyping. If you say you're from Jane and Finch, people look at you in a different way.

If you have Jane and Finch on your resume, you aren't going to get hired. I have to lie about where I live if I want to get a job. If you live in

Jane and Finch, people go, "Oh." They already judge you and think you're a bad person. You come from that neighbourhood so you're not good.

Other than that, I'd say the community is pretty good. People here help one another.

◆

I've lived around the area ever since I was three years old. Initially, I lived on Jane Street, just south of Sheppard Avenue, then moved to a house minutes away from C. W. Jeffreys. For years, my big connection to Jane-Finch was the Jane-Finch Mall. As a child, I would either go there with my parents or ride my bike. The big draw for me was the Towers department store. I remember going there to buy record albums (I just dated myself, didn't I?), toys, and pipe tobacco for my father.

When Towers and Food City went out of business, their locations were combined to create a massive K-Mart. That store didn't last too long. I always liked having a major department store close to home.

In the early 1990s, I spoke with a woman who lived in an apartment building near York University. When I mentioned the Jane-Finch Mall, she said that she never went there because it was too dangerous. That surprised me. I've never felt unsafe at that mall.

After Yorkgate Mall opened across the street, their Zellers became my one stop shopping destination over the last decade. It got to the point where I was there at least once a week, often more. When the Zellers' chain went out of business, I attended the store closing sales at other locations, but not once did I go to the Yorkgate Mall. It felt like I would be taking advantage of a friend's hardship. In the year or so since Zellers left, I may have gone to Yorkgate Mall two or three times.

I'm glad that the Shoppers Drug Mart in the Jane-Finch Mall has expanded and invested money to make the store look better. I think retail is an important barometer of a community's health and outlook. Clean, vibrant, prosperous shops make me feel good, even if I have lessened my reliance on retail therapy.

◆

I've been living in Jane-Finch since 1985. Before that, I lived in the east end, but can't remember too much because I've been here a long time. After that, we lived on Vaughan Road. We went to live on Wilson Avenue right by the subway. This was when they were building the subway, so that was around 1977. We went back to Vaughan Road, then Arlington. After that, we came to Jane and Woolner.

In 1985, I was living at 10 San Romanoway - it was a very bad place then. I had friends who didn't want to park their cars down there when they came to visit. It was also bad when I was living at Woolner. The police were always on that street. Even when I was living on Oakwood, around Marlee, those places were bad. And what happened at Marlee was the same thing that happened here.

When things changed, they changed a lot. When you went to San Romanoway, you had to have a job that paid over thirty thousand to get an apartment there. When I got there, it was thirty-two thousand, because my husband and I together had that. Otherwise, you couldn't get a two bedroom apartment. They realized to move the bad people out, they had to raise the rent. And it worked. Because when I went there to live, it was good.

But one thing started going on after a while - three people can get together and rent a three bedroom apartment. I moved out when that started to happen. So it's the things they do badly that cause these problems again. Because you see, it's getting bad. I had to move away because I was getting scared to go out at night.

I went to live in an apartment in the Jane-Shoreham area, near the plaza. There was bad management. Some people who lived there wouldn't pay rent as a way to complain. They didn't give me back my key money, which was twenty-five dollars. They still have it, thirty years later. I would never again move into an apartment that asks for key money. The rent was around $200 a month.

It was a nice apartment but it was not well kept. I gave them six weeks notice, but they still kept the key money. If I knew they would keep the money, I would have kept the keys.

Then I moved down to an apartment building in the Jane and Firgrove Crescent area. The one thing I miss from that building is the air conditioning. It also had the best heating - you could control it.

Otherwise, I found the apartment wasn't that good. Things were happening in my apartment once a new superintendent came. We had an alarm, and it was broken. The owner didn't want me to leave but I couldn't stay. The building that I moved into now has twenty-four hour security. I would still live in Jane-Finch, but I think I have given it a try. I lived there over twenty years. I still come to the area.

◆

I came to Jane-Finch thirty years ago after having just got married in Egypt. I didn't know the English language along with not having any friends or family with me. I always used to cry because I was alone with nobody with me for the first couple of years.

I always used to be at the balcony watching for whenever my husband would return home. Standing there in the balcony I was always so fascinated with the new habitat I'd be living in for the rest of my life.

What really shocked me was how the people here in Canada hugged and kissed the other sex. Back home in Egypt you would never see something like that happen.

When the winter arrived, I was so shocked by the cold that I didn't even want to get out of my house. One day, I stepped out to go get some groceries from the local food market. I felt the cold and never wanted to walk out in the open with that weather ever again.

My husband eventually bought a used car. To this day, he drives me everywhere to go shopping because of the shock I was in when I first felt the winter weather. The weather in Canada will be one thing that I'll never forget for my whole life.

◆

Jane-Finch is a beautiful neighbourhood where a lot of tragedy takes place. Many bad things take place and anything can happen to you on any given day. You say it's a beautiful place but people from the outside come in and destroy the people on the inside.

Notes

[1] When residents refer to "Chalkfarm," they mean the four towers located at the southern edge of Chalkfarm Drive, a residential crescent west off Jane Street, and moments north of Wilson Avenue.

[2] Black Creek Community Health Centre: "a non-profit, community based organization that provides health care services in a holistic manner and works with people to create safe and healthy communities" (description from their web site, http://www.bcchc.com/).

[3] Jane/Finch Community and Family Centre: "a community based organization driven by passion, innovation, and a strong commitment to social justice, community engagement and collaboration" (description from their web site, http://www.janefinchcentre.org/).

My Story - One (Female)

"I keep a lot inside."

I came from Egypt in July 1984, and I got married in Canada. The marriage was arranged in Egypt. My husband-to-be was living here. His mother was working with my aunt's husband. My aunt lived here, and his whole family was living in Canada. His mother asked my aunt if they had a girl for his son.

My father was dead, and he divorced my mother when I was five months old. My mother married another man when I was six. When my father died, he was very rich and I found out he left everything to his second wife, and he didn't have any children with her. This left me very stressed, as I only had a little bit of money. So I was having a very difficult time when my aunt called my mother to ask if I would go to Canada and marry this man.

They said he doesn't smoke, he doesn't drink, he's religious. So I said, "Okay, let me go." His father came to Egypt and married me in place of his son. This was what we did when you married someone who lived outside the country. So I never met my husband before we married. I saw his photograph. Later, I realized they sent me a picture of him when he was younger.

When I came to Canada, my aunt took me straight from the airport to her place. When my aunt met me at the airport, I was very sick, I couldn't speak English, and I was very cold. I was dressed for summer in Egypt.

When I got to my aunt's place, I kept throwing up. My aunt called my mother-in-law and told her I was here. They got very upset, saying, "Why didn't you tell us so we could get her from the airport?" My aunt said this is what my mother wanted, to stay in my aunt's place for one week.

My husband came to visit me at my aunt's place. When I saw him, he looked so old. I didn't want to go with him to see the apartment where we were going to live. My cousin came with me, and we saw it. There was very nice furniture.

To tell the truth, I didn't like him. I called my mother and cried, asking if I could go back home. "He's ugly and he's old!"

He was just five years older than me, but he looked so old. My mother said, "Too late, he's your husband, you can't come back, you have to marry him." My aunt made a white dress for me. Every woman who saw me said, "You're beautiful, but he's so ugly!"

In my culture, you don't tell the girl anything about sex. Everything about sex was "Shame, shame, shame." I'm not allowed to put on make-up, not allowed to do my eyebrows, not allowed to laugh on the street because I'm a girl. My husband didn't know much more. The first month we were married, he kept asking me why I wasn't pregnant yet. He hadn't touched me! I told my aunt about it, and she said, "Is he stupid? How can you be pregnant if he hasn't touched you yet!"

My aunt told her husband. He phoned my husband and said, "How can she be pregnant? Why didn't you tell me to bring you a lady who was already pregnant if you wanted a baby?"

I got pregnant after the first time he touched me. How did I find out? I was at my mother-in-law's one day. The cigarette smoke made me throw up. My mother-in-law said I was probably pregnant.

She wasn't happy about my being pregnant and said I had to get an abortion. She had been nagging me to have a baby. They paid a specialist $250 to do the procedure. Before the operation, I had to sign a release. I couldn't speak English, so I didn't understand why they wanted me to sign a paper. I was afraid they wanted to kill me, so I didn't sign.

So I didn't have the operation. When I told my husband, he said, "I'll give you the operation right now." He put my arms behind my back and he kicked me in my stomach. He beat me and said, "I'll make the baby come out now."

He made all the water come down and I had to go to the hospital. They had to put me in a bed for one week with my legs up. I got an epidural to make water for the baby. Before that, he used to call me names, beat me, and slap me. It was very bad. I said "Enough is enough, I can't stay with him."

The first time he beat me, I called the police. They didn't do anything. The police were stupid back then (1984), not like now. He said he didn't do anything and they believed him.

He wouldn't buy me food. All we ever ate were potatoes - I had to make French fries, mashed potatoes, potatoes with tomato sauce. No meat, no chicken, no nothing. I'd ask for watermelon or mango, he'd say it was too expensive. Back where I came from, we always ate fresh fruit, because it wasn't expensive for us.

I only stayed with him for four months. I left while I was still pregnant. We got divorced and I went to stay with my aunt for four months. Her husband didn't want the baby to disturb his sleep, so I left them before I had my child.

Next, I rented a room from an Italian woman. It was $350. The welfare came and gave me $550 because I was an immigrant here. My landlady was very nice to me at first. I was afraid to be alone. I spent a lot of time crying and she would come and ask me upstairs. Later she became the devil. Whenever she left the house, she'd unplug the phone so I couldn't call anyone.

When I had my child, I was happy. Then I had a gall bladder attack, and had to go to the hospital. No one knew what was wrong at first, and I stayed there for 40 days. They gave me morphine so I couldn't breast feed. My baby got his own room.

The hospital told me he had to leave because it was costing $350 a day to give him his own room. I told them I would leave with my baby. The social worker came and tried to explain, and I told them I wasn't sick when I came to Canada. My baby stayed. A Spanish doctor figured out it was my gall bladder. I got back to the house, and the landlady told me she needed the room for her son.

I called the social worker and she said it was short notice so I had to go to a downtown shelter. It was a very dirty shelter, I don't remember the name of it. In the room, I only had a bed, a crib, and a mirror. The government sent a van to take all my furniture and store it some place. They couldn't speak Egyptian, but I had a friend who translated for me.

What I saw in that shelter was all new to me. The first time I saw a man and a woman kissing in the street, I got scared. I thought I had to call the police for that. They told me it was normal and that surprised me. In the shelter's TV room, I'd see a man kiss his wife and it made me sick, made me want to throw up. I had to stay in my room. I didn't want to go downstairs, I didn't want to see that again.

I stayed in my room until I got weak. All the food was pork, so I had to eat salad. For breakfast, there was cereal which I never ate before. They called a doctor who said I lost a lot of weight.

They also got a social worker to help me. She was a good lady. She took me and my baby to the park, took pictures of us, she tried to make me happy, and she asked me what I wanted. I said, "I don't want to stay here in the shelter. I don't like what I see here - I won't go downstairs and see people touching and kissing each other."

I didn't want to go back to my native country. I was already married and divorced, my life was going to be so miserable there. I wouldn't be allowed to wear nice clothes, I wouldn't be allowed to go out on the balcony, not allowed to laugh: "Oh, you're divorced! You have to stay inside!" They would treat me very bad.

I was sent to a woman's only shelter on Albion Road. It was very nice. There were no men. The room had two beds and two cribs. I stayed with a nice Italian lady and her baby. Each person had to cook for the whole house. I told the worker I didn't want to cook for everyone and vice versa. Their food was not the same as my food. So they called a meeting and everyone said what they wanted to eat. There was a freezer filled with meat. I took a big piece. They threw out the leftover, and that shocked me. It wasn't that I was cheap, it was against my religion to throw out good food. I asked them to give me a smaller piece.

The wife of the iman of my mosque helped me get into public housing and I got my first choice. It was October 1985. The first apartment I saw, I loved it. I wanted to get out of the shelter. The welfare brought back my furniture. I was so happy to get my own place. When I got the key, I was jumping up and down. I didn't know anyone in the building.

When the baby got older, I used to go work at a bakery making sweets. I was paid under the table. One day, someone called my social worker. She told me someone told her I was working, and gave her an address. I was lucky I was home when the phone rang, and I told her I wasn't working because I would have lost everything. How could I afford diapers and the milk and the special soap? I only ate potatoes and hot peppers. They only gave me $200 for food. The baby bonus was thirty-two dollars. I enjoyed whatever I had. Back then, I didn't know about food banks. I don't use canned food. I like to buy fresh vegetables.

I put my child in day care. I went to Oakdale Middle School for a couple of years. They told me to get tested at Emery Collegiate Institute. The test took a few hours, and they told me I was at a Grade Nine level. Some classes I took with adults, and some classes I took with the Grade Nine students.

The government gave me a Metropass. I would drop my son off at Palisades Day Care, then take the Finch bus, get off at Weston Road and walk to Emery. I'd be there the whole day.

I promised myself I would never touch my kids. My mother used to beat me. I never sent my children to breakfast programs because I was afraid Children's Aid Society would come and ask me what I was doing with the welfare money, because I wasn't giving my children breakfast.

Back then, I hated all the men in the world. My ex-husband never came to see his son. I stayed alone for ten years. I went back to my old country and found my second husband. I fell in love with him and he came to Canada in 1995. My husband and I didn't get along. He left when my second child was two or three years old. After that, I said, "That's it! I won't get married again."

I got divorced two years ago in the Canadian way. Later, I got back together with my husband in the religious way. Relatives told me he would never change, but I defended him, saying he did change and was treating me like a queen. He'd make me tea after supper. If I was tired, he would do the dishes. He mopped the floor because he was a very clean man. We were back together about eight months.

We visited Saudi Arabia and stayed at a hotel in separate rooms. I don't know why he came. He never helped me there. One day, my friend asked me to help her get a cart for her daughter. I went outside the hotel and there was my husband sitting with another man. He said to me, "What are you doing out here? Go inside!"

I told him to be quiet and he got mad and wanted to beat me. The other man said, "Don't touch her! Do you think you're going to beat her here?"

My husband said, "No, I just want to talk to her." And he called me every bad word in the book. I told him to stop it. We didn't talk after that. We didn't even get on the airplane together.

When we got back to Canada, I called him. He said he was still at the airport and to leave him alone. I tried calling him, leaving messages.

Finally, I got hold of him.

He said, "You know what? I don't want to see you, I don't want to see your face! Don't call me any more!" But he was so nice to me before. What happened?

He asked if I remembered the time I told him to be quiet? For him, that was a big deal. Months later, my son called him to ask what happened. He told him it was because I told him to be quiet. That was it. I don't see him any more. That's how stupid the men from my country can be!

When I think of how my husband treated me, I ask myself, "Why do I put myself down for a person like that?" For what? Do I need a man to talk to? It's not what the people think.

I need a man for a lot more than just to be husband and wife, I need him to be a friend. To find somebody who is there for me, to tell me, "Oh, don't worry, tomorrow it will be better, you will be healthy" - stuff like that. I explained to my kids when they got upset that I went back to him. My kids were right and I was wrong to go back to him.

It hurt when my kids didn't want me to go back with him; it hurt from everybody who told me that. Many times I don't show it. Many people, my neighbours, they'll say, "Oh, you're always happy," because I always laugh.

But it doesn't mean that the laughter comes from my heart - you don't know what is inside. I keep a lot inside. That's why I see a psychologist every week to talk about my problems.

To tell you the truth, I can't tell her everything because she writes everything down. One time I told her I felt tired and I didn't want to wake up. She said, "Oh, did you want to kill yourself?" Does she think I am crazy - if I said yes, she wouldn't let me walk out the door. She would call the police!

I would never think of killing myself. Instead, I pray to God to keep me alive until I can see my children's kids and see them finish university. When I cook for my children, I feel happy because I'm doing something for them that they like.

The Finch hospital helped me with both of my pregnancies. Thank God it was close by. After my first husband beat me and made all the water come down, they had to put me in bed for ten days for my first pregnancy. Thank God I didn't lose my baby.

This is what happened fifteen years ago while I was carrying my second child. Someone was knocking very hard on my door and it scared me. I tried to open the door but I had a small carpet in front of my door. The carpet tripped my legs and I went down on my stomach. But I wasn't smart enough and I didn't go to the hospital. The next day, I felt the baby play a little less and less. The third day I didn't feel the baby play at all. I got scared.

When my husband got home from work, I made a big breakfast. After we ate, he said, "Don't make me tea because I'm going to sleep." I said, "You're not going to sleep. The baby's not playing, you have to take me to the hospital."

At the hospital, they said I only had half an hour before my baby and I would die. The cord was blocked and he wasn't getting blood. They had to open me like a watermelon. The baby had problems with his heart, his liver, his kidneys, and he needed blood. They had to take him to Women's College Hospital because they didn't have any blood for him. Neither SickKids Hospital or Toronto General Hospital would take him, and they talked about getting a plane and taking him to another country, but Women's College took him. For ten days, I was in the hospital here at Jane-Finch while he was at Women's College. It was difficult, but at least the hospital was here to help me and deliver my baby.

I'm happy, but I'm very sick. I'm supposed to have a knee operation, but my doctor says I'm still young. I went to have my knee cleaned, and they damaged my knee. A specialist sent me for x-rays and the bones are not together. I can't walk. I find work as a translator, because I still like to help people, and do different things for my community.

I would like to have a man in my life to make me feel like a woman, to bring out my soft side. Instead I have to be hard all the time. As a single mother, I have to be the man and the woman. All my life I don't feel a man ever helped me financially.

I always tell my children that everybody deserves to get respect, even the people on the street that they don't know. My mother and my religion taught me that. If someone on the street I don't know says, "hi," I smile and say, "How are you? How have you been?"

That's what I teach my children. If they see an old lady, they'll help her open the door, help carry the bags.

Comments from her two sons:
(Her eldest son) Certainly, my mother never let me lack for anything. She sacrificed a lot for me. Here's an example: she wore a spring jacket for four winters because she wanted to purchase the latest things for me. I always had the best shoes, the best clothes, and I think that was detrimental to her health. She now suffers from rheumatoid arthritis, and that came from the cold affecting her joints. That's something I've always appreciated.

(Her younger son) My mother is an inspiring figure. She gave up a lot for us. For example, she was going to summer school to get her high school degree and was in her last year when she got pregnant. She pretty much gave up her life for us. She denies herself things so she can save money for my future needs, like tuition. She never puts herself first.

Intolerance

How does it feel to be singled out because of your skin colour, religious beliefs, accent, or hair style? It can happen anywhere.

When I go to a mall with a friend, security will stereotype and start looking at us like we're going to steal. Personally, I don't steal so when the workers stare at me for so long, I'll start to feel, what the hell, is this because I'm black? Is that why they're looking at me? It makes no sense.

But that's just certain stores, it's not all the stores. I look like I'm in high school but I'm not in high school anymore. So they put me in that category, thinking I'm ready to steal. But I don't have time for that because I'm over eighteen. If I steal and get caught, it goes on my record which is not a really pleasant outcome for me. My goal is to do something in criminology.

How do I feel about this kind of discrimination? I feel hurt. It's because I'm black and if I was white, would I feel this way? Would I get this much attention? The attention that I want I don't get, the attention that I get I don't want. I get attention for the wrong reasons.

◆

I didn't know what racism was until I lived in Jane-Finch. To me, it was a word I hadn't heard before. Someone explained it to me, and that's when I understood what I had been experiencing. In Jamaica, we experienced segregation. I lived in the city and what I saw was white people living in the rich neighbourhood, the brown people living in the second richest neighbourhood, and us poor ones living in the poor area. So I was used to a class system.

When I went to the U.S.A. once, that's when I really saw segregation, and I never want to go back there. Here, we're more blended. In Canada, we see white people on the bus.

Being brown at home (Jamaica), you'd get the cat eye. You still get that negativity here in Canada, but you're more accepted. It's what my father says, "When you're white, you're right; when you're brown, you can hang around; and when you're black, get back!"

◆

Let's talk about demographics. There are many races when you come out to Jane and Finch but when I look at it personally and see who has the jobs, they all look very white. And when you go into the factories and all that, the other nations will get multiples of them. When you see who works the part-time shifts, what does it look like at those places? You see older white people, because they need the money too.

◆

The flooding (July 8, 2013) filled my basement with water up to my knees. A lot of stuff was ruined. I found one box that wasn't damaged. Inside it, I found a clipping of an article from the Share newspaper. The story was nearly twenty years old. The story was about me.

I was at Wal-Mart with my son, who was three or four at the time. There was an announcement that the store was closing for the night. I was making my way out, only my son ran off back to the toy section. I was going aisle to aisle, calling him, but he was not responding. I figured he'd be around the toy cars, because that's what he loved.

I was approached by a plainclothes security guard. He said, "Are you deaf? Are you deaf? Can't you hear we're closed?"

I said, "I understand that. I'm just going to get my son."

He replied, "Oh no, you're not. Are you deaf? You black bitch, what do I have to do to get through to you?"

So I said, "I'm not leaving the store without my son," who was only a couple of aisles over. The security stood there and wouldn't get out of my way. I stepped aside to pass him by, and he said, "You little black bitch," and he went on to make special slurs, "It's people like you who are so ignorant, you don't know anything."

By then, his voice got really loud and he grabbed my wrist and was twisting it. I was saying, "Let me go," and another plainclothes security came by and said, "It's bitches like them that always give trouble."

At that time, my son saw everything that happened. He was so scared that he ran to the guard grabbing my arm and said, "Let my mommy go!"

That guard took his other hand and pushed my son, who fell and he banged his forehead against one of the metal shelves holding toys.

The security said, "You'd better get out, and furthermore, you're banned from this store and you're banned from the mall."

They escorted me out.

My son was just beyond himself. He was hurt by this big muscular guy who he saw grab his mother. I went home and called an ambulance because I was concerned about the head injury. They said I should look further into it.

I did press charges on the gentleman. Dudley Laws[1] took up this case, and that's when I met him for the first time. Somebody introduced him to me. I remember doing an interview with him. Then the Share newspaper called me as well. I went to their offices and told them my story.

For myself, it wasn't what I wanted as a mother, I just wanted the gentleman to apologize to my son. After that, my son was afraid of all big white muscular gentlemen. I had him go to counselling.

It was a battle back and forth, and Dudley and other activists were trying to communicate with Wal-Mart on our behalf. They also picketed that Wal-Mart location. Wal-Mart said these men weren't Wal-Mart staff, and they didn't have to let them work there. Wal-Mart said they had good staff, and they didn't think it was that bad. Mr. Laws was able to talk to the top man at Wal-Mart, and I was supposed to get an apology. They ended up firing that guard. My son doesn't remember it, which I guess I'm happy about.

Seeing that article brought it all back - the smell of the store, the look on that guard's face. It still hurts me the same, because what else is a mother to do but to go get her child? The guard also accused me of stealing, which was crazy because I was in the middle of the aisle, not near anything. Now I'm a bitch, I'm a whore, I'm a thief, just for trying to get my son. The experience was really awful.

◆

I have faced many discriminatory insults being thrown at me blatantly. Being of Muslim decent, I was always being discriminated against because of my traditional headwear, the hijab. Wearing it gives away that you're a Muslim. Even with the hardships, I still stayed true to my religion in wearing the hijab and not letting anyone see my skin and hair.

◆

I've brought my children to my workplace, off and on. The last time, I brought my teenagers there and they were called "cute monkeys." This was just last year. I said to myself, "You know what? It's one thing that I have to enjoy this but there's no way I'm going to dress my kids to go there so that they'll have to question me after the fact, asking me, what did those people mean?"

This happened at another job too, where my supervisor asked me, "How are your little monkeys doing?"

◆

I'm in somewhat of an unique position in this community. I don't come from the black community, but many people perceive me as possibly being black or a visible minority. When the community discusses young males who come from single parent households, such as myself, a lot of the emphasis centers on black males. As someone who doesn't necessarily identify with black males, but certainly identifies as a racialized male, I've always felt, not to say cheated, but I've felt some frustration around that. There are other racialized males, and other minorities who also have needs, yet the dialogue is always around black males. Growing up, it seemed that even organizations would target programs towards black males and not other males.

◆

My mother's father was Indian, and my mother's mother was a mix of Indian, black, and Spanish. My grandfather was Scottish. People told me I had "Chinese eyes," especially when I was a child. My son has these "Chinese eyes" too.

I was born in Kingston and spoke Patois. That changed when I came to Canada, because people couldn't understand what I was saying. All I'd hear from them was, "Pardon me?" Now my Patois is gone, and I don't want to learn it again.

◆

Where I currently work, sometimes I can't believe it's 2014 going by what rolls out of the mouths of people on a daily basis. They are some of the most racist people - they just have Jamaicans in such a bubble and yet they always travel to that country for their vacations. I don't get it - we're such evil, uneducated monstrous people and all we do is have babies with as many different men as we can, yet every vacation you want to suntan there or ask us about our food and culture.

There's always some kind of stereotyping going on where I work. If a black educated client comes in, and staff are talking about their life and their education, and the client says, "Yes, my children are in university," the staff will say, "How can you afford that?"

There was one gentleman who had six children and he said that his last one was finishing university; in fact, all six had gone and the other five were working in their fields. One employee's response was, "Are all six of those kids from the same baby mother? You know how you Jamaican men like to have kids from all different women."

The gentleman's jaw just dropped. This is how freely our staff speaks on a daily basis. I can't believe I'm working in a professional office.

◆

I tell my kids, "I'm Jamaican-Canadian because I was born in Jamaica, but you're Canadian." People ask me where I'm from, and I'll say Canada, because it's where I live. Then they follow up, "Where were you born?"

So then I understand, and I'll say "Jamaica." And I wonder why are they asking me? Would they be asking this if I was white?

◆

The dynamics at my workplace changed. I was the "black girl" and the only black girl. Then I was off, and when I returned, I found they had hired another black woman. They feel that this position can only be filled by a minority. You can't work front desk, you can't be one-to-one dealing with clients, you're in the back and you're the voice that no one knows who you are. If someone comes by looking for you and bringing something for you, they'll get so upset, they won't speak to you for the rest of the day - "How dare you leave the back and go speak with people." It's such a brainwashed negative system.

Now that there's two of us, and the dynamic has shifted. I think it was easy to pick on me because I was the only one. Now people will ask questions, such as, "Were you offended by that?"

They try to tip toe around the racism a little bit because there are two of us now. If there was any doubt in the other woman's mind, that's gone. She'll say, "This place is very racist, is it not?"

Someone once told me that there had been over forty coloured women in my position. They will not hire any other nationality because the workload is too much, and they feel that this is for "us" to do. Normally, there's one receptionist for three professionals. In my position, I'm the receptionist for seven professionals, so the workload is not equal. I'll mention this to the owners, and they'll say, "We don't see what you're talking about." I guess that's why those forty others all left.

I am looking for another position, but I won't leave until I have something first. I feel if I can last here, there's no place I can work that will take me over. Many people have come here and just broken. There have been people who only lasted a day here, some who lasted a week. Because I was raised in another province that was so much more racist, so completely racist, I think I have developed a second skin.

I'm not saying that what they're doing is right, it's just that I'm not easily broken. If I break, I'm breaking myself. I'll never give you that power over me. I think they just know I'm a tough cookie.

I even get it from clients who call over the phone. "Are you the Italian girl?" I'll give them my name. "Oh, you're the black girl. Give me the Italian one. She speaks Italian."

So I'll reply, "Excuse me, but your English was very good right now, you did an excellent job of articulating yourself, so you can continue in the same kind of English and I'm sure I can be the one to help you out."

I remember one time a black client was late bringing his child in for an appointment. We're only talking fifteen minutes. He apologized for it. Things broke off, and suddenly the four staff were speaking Italian, going back and forth. That gentleman stood there listening. Finally, he turned around and said, "It's funny. If I were to talk about your mothers the way you just talked about my mother, you wouldn't like it too much."

I believe he came from Somalia. Obviously, he understood Italian. I couldn't stop laughing! I had to put a client on hold. That man just blasted them. Later, these women turned to me and asked why I didn't say anything. What was I supposed to say? How could I know he understood Italian?

"Well, you're black and he was black, so you're all supposed to relate."

Since I was four, I grew up with best friends who were Italian. And their parents treated us as if there was no difference between any of us. My parents are your parents, and vice versa. You're in trouble, I'm in trouble, you're fed, I'm fed. I'd tell this to the Italians at work, and they'd look at me as if to say, "Oh hell no."

I've met the parents of one of these workers, and I can only wonder, "How did your daughter get this way?" The parents are so nice and loving that I want to wrap them up and take them home. They talk about their struggles coming to Canada, the good friends they've made who are also minorities, and I'll think that somewhere along the way, their kids lost it. I don't know where their racism is coming from, when their parents are so pro-minority. The parents say, "If you close your eyes, we're all one." Then I'm working with this person whose attitude is "I'm up here and you're down there by my feet."

That's what gets me. It's better when I know exactly what you think of me rather than you're trying to fake your way through it. I can still get the job done around you. You don't have to like me, but if I've got the job, I'll still come in and get it done. I just can't change everybody.

The funny thing, well it's not funny, is that the place where I work is listed on a site. Go on that site and you'll see people have left comments on how the staff is very racist. It's known. You can feel it.

Within the week that I was hired, they told me, "See? We're not racist - we hired you." Wow, I thought it was my skills and education that got me the job, not that I'm some special charity case. What I don't understand is that most of the clients are minorities. These are the people your paychecks depend on - how can you act this way towards them? It's an eye opener for me.

◆

If you fight people over racist remarks, you won't get anywhere with them. If it's bad, you have to stand up. Otherwise, ignore it and be nice. You can win over a lot of people.

◆

Going back to my school days, one thing I noticed was that white kids got bullied the most. I don't know if it was some kind of reverse racism, but they got the most abuse. They'd be called "honky," "hick," "trailer park trash," and they would get bullied, both boys and girls.

I've long maintained that the white people who live in this community are among the most disadvantaged. Because of the perceived social privilege that people think they have, people will think that because they're white, they have all these opportunities.

But often that's not the case. They're living in social housing, so they're low income, but they can't access equal employment opportunities because they're white. At the same time, they're the minorities in the schools here. They're treated like crap, actually. If there was a white boy in the class, you'd call him "white boy," but if that white boy called someone "black boy" or "Indian boy" or "Muslim boy," you know that there would be some serious repercussions.

Thinking about it now, when you're in middle school, you don't really understand colonialism or those kinds of things, so I wonder if the kids were picking this up at home from their parents or older siblings? Who expects a twelve year old to make those kinds of comments?

◆

There was a time, when I was speaking to a woman at work, and one of the other staff came by. He said, "Really? You're from Jamaica?," probably with the assumption that I was born here because of the way I speak. She answered for me, because I had told her about my childhood and how my mother was raised by a British family that lived in Jamaica. She answered saying, "The reason she doesn't speak like those people is that her mother was raised right." I just had to look at her and say, "Yeah, I guess you cleared that up really well."

◆

Whenever a black person commits a crime, you always hear "send them back to where they came from." Nowadays, we send some money back home just in case we get kicked out. This is why Western Union is getting rich. With all this talk, now we know that we do not belong here.

◆

I get a lot of "you people" questions. Do "you people" eat this? Do "you people" go here? Do "you people" always (fill in the blank)? I'm still waiting to know who the "you people" are!

◆

One thing that is being brought into our society that we don't realize as being rather dangerous is being labeled as a multicultural society. The problem with multiculturalism is that it replaces individual identity. For example, I could be in a class that's said to be a "multicultural" class. What does that mean? We're not homogenous, we're not all the same.

There's differences of gender, disability, social class, race, and so on. Everyone's reality is different, and there are different barriers to be faced.

"Multicultural" replaces "identity" and exerts the narrative that we're all the same in a melting pot. People may not think of it, but saying we live in a multicultural society is a regression in many ways.

The "multicultural" label tries to assimilate everyone into a melting pot, but the problem is that in reality, society doesn't operate like that. In reality, certain groups have self-identities and have barriers. If you try to assimilate them, you disregard their barriers. For example, someone who has a disability has systemic barriers and disadvantages that the rest of us might not have. That's where it becomes an issue. In theory, the term is just used for culture, but in practice it's being used to label everything. It disregards disabilities, it disregards everything that makes us individuals. The intentions may have been good, but who recalls that old saying about good intentions and which road they pave?

◆

One of my sisters has a phobia about dogs. When we were growing up in Manitoba during the late 1980s, there was one particular dog in our neighbourhood named N****r. Its owner trained it to attack black people.

Because my sister was the slowest runner out of all of us, she always got bitten by the dog. To this day, if you have a dog as small as your hand, my sister is terrified. She has such a phobia because of all the dog bites.

Nowadays, if a dog bites you, you're a millionaire. Back then, it was just another wound we had to clean, another rip in her dress. The owner would just say, "What are you talking about? It wasn't our dog. Can you prove it?"

My parents approached them the nice way, because they lived on our street. We had to come home after school every single day, and the owner would say, "N****r, get 'em!"

You could be in a mixed group, and that dog would only go after people of colour. When we called the police, they said we had to find alternative routes to and from school because that was the dog's home. In their eyes, maybe it was us aggravating the dog.

I feel badly for my sister because that's something that has stuck with her forever. We could be walking down the street and she'll fly out into traffic if she sees a dog on the sidewalk. It takes a toll on her - she can't breathe, she'll cry, she loses herself, you have to grab her from running into the street.

You'll still get called the n-word in Manitoba in 2013. It's still very easy rolling off the lips I would say compared to Ontario. I went back there in 2010, and somebody walked right up to me at the back of the bus and said, "Why don't you N****rs go right back to where you come from? You're still coming to our country? What the hell?"

I was stunned. My kids are used to being in schools where they're the majority, schools where they have a black principal, and this kind of talk is just not seen or heard, so they were shocked. My dad says his car gets damaged and vandalized. He lives in an area where he's very much in the minority. The car will get stolen, and sometimes spray painted, "Get out of town." He's retired and this is what he still has to put up with there in Manitoba. He's been there since the 1970s.

I tell him it's not that much different here in Toronto. People won't come to your doorstep and say "I hate you," but they'll try every other way, hoping you'll get the message.

◆

A woman told me, if you want to get a job here, you've got to get straighter hair. It's my hair that makes me black.

◆

The other thing about my workplace is that they want to discuss all black crimes with me. They'll ask if I heard about a crime, and if I didn't, they'll say I'm lying.

One day, I saw a drug bust in the Jane-Finch area. I was approaching the Jane-Finch Mall, coming down one of the side streets. It was huge, there were many police vans, there was only one lane to drive along when we were allowed to move. Because the traffic was so slowed down, I got to see what was going on.

The police even had battering rams to break down doors. This street was lined with houses, and the police had broken down the doors of all these houses next to each other. The police were taking people out, and they were all white youth who the police were putting into the vans. Their mothers were coming out, speaking their different languages, saying "Don't take my son away!"

So I told this story at work, but I didn't mention that the youths were white. They said, "It's Jane-Finch! Those black kids are always selling dope." When I said they were all white, the staff got so upset, saying stuff like, "That's a lie!"

Crime happens in all communities and all cultures. People need to stop the colour coding. People are dying, people are being robbed, people are suffering - it's just people. Once you give people titles, then you start to make excuses for why behaviour is as it is, why people do what they do.

If I come up to you and say a person robbed me, then it's the robbery that's bad and you focus on the robbery. If I say a black person robbed me, then it becomes, "Why did the black guy do that? He probably needed drugs," and we start to break everything down instead of thinking, "Oh my gosh, you got robbed!"

Stop putting labels on people and you'll make better decisions on how to deal with people and how people interact.

◆

After 9/11, things got difficult for Muslims. That's not a priority in an area like Jane-Finch where the racial minority tends to be black or Hispanic. The oppression they face takes precedent over other groups. Everyone faces different things. No one ever wonders how it feels to be a Muslim man walking through an airport nowadays.

I can't grow a beard because I'll be perceived as a radical. Going to a doctor's office knowing my name is going to be called out makes me anxious. I don't look like the typical Muslim (whatever that is), so I get nervous that my name will single me out.

The community doesn't look at the bigger picture. The reality is no oppression takes place in isolation. That's how you divide and conquer.

Prior to the last U.S. election, I was watching Republican debates on TV. The question came up, what are you going to do about Muslim terrorism? Herman Cain said we need to give local authorities discretion to profile Muslims.[2] He wanted to reserve the right to strip citizenship from Muslims. He got a standing ovation. That didn't even make the news. Here you had a black man, not far removed from the civil rights movement, saying this about another group.

◆

There's a sense of being unwanted. It's how you're treated by a whole system. I remember going to school when I first came here, and the teacher looked at me and said, "You can't take advanced math." I asked why, and she told me she didn't think I could do it. I was already eighteen, so I said, "Listen, even if I fail, I'm going to take advanced math." I ended up getting a C, but don't tell me what I can and what I cannot do. Every kid that came from the Caribbean got put back, even if they were getting A's back home.

◆

Growing up and going into school, I had issues because I wasn't black, I wasn't Vietnamese, I wasn't Hispanic - those were the dominant groups. However, a lot of people thought I looked mixed. The black and Hispanic girls all liked me. The black guys would hate me because I was lighter, and the Spanish guys would hate me for being darker.

◆

When people ask me about issues facing Jane-Finch and Toronto in general, I think back to one day back in August 2006. I was helping a candidate for City Council in the municipal election. She was told about a community party taking place next to the Oakdale Community Centre.[3]

I agreed to go and arrived just as the party was starting. I offered to work one barbecue, and was put in charge of the hot dogs. This made me very popular with the children, and I had a steady stream of hungry customers to joke around with as I worked the grill. It was a lot of fun, and I think there may have been close to three hundred people present.

The candidate wouldn't show up until the party was nearly over, some five or six hours later. However, about ninety minutes into the event, one of her campaign volunteers dropped by. He pulled me aside and lowered his voice.

"Aren't you afraid to be here?" he asked.

Afraid? Why? I was having a great time.

"You're the only white person here."

Really? I looked around. By this time, the crowd would have been at its peak. True, I was the only pale skin in a sea of smiling faces.

"I guess I've been having too much fun to notice," I replied.

"Really? I'm black and I feel nervous being here," he replied. I'd like to think he was joking, but I knew he lived outside Toronto.

He soon left, and I went back to my grill. Now that my eyes had been opened to the racial reality, I made it a point to look for pale faces within the crowd. If any other white people made an appearance during the event, I certainly didn't see them. At no point did anyone make me feel uncomfortable - in fact, some people went out of their way to make me feel part of the party.

After a while, it bothered me. This party was being held in a courtyard located in Yorkwoods Village facing Grandravine Drive. To the east, only a few hundred metres away, was Driftwood Avenue, lined with houses, with many more in the sub-division behind it. I know many of those house owners are white. Driftwood Avenue is only two lanes wide, but on that day, that strip of asphalt felt like a chasm between two worlds.

To get back to my opening sentence, I believe Jane-Finch and Toronto in general needs to bring people together on a social level. I don't think we'll make meaningful improvements until we know each other as people, and not as separate groups, stereotypes, or numbers on a spreadsheet.

◆

Seven or eight years ago, a friend of mine was working at a hotel. Her employers told her to take off her scarf or we'll fire you. She was working at the front. She was a beautiful women who wore makeup, so I don't know why there was a problem with her looks. She had to resign.

We need employers to recognize the requirements of our Muslim faith. We need breaks for prayer. I appreciate that most stores now sell halal meats.

◆

"There's no racism in Canada." So said a fellow white co-worker a few years ago. So I told him about my personal reality check in 2004.

That's when an ex-flame contacted me to go for lunch. We broke up two years earlier, and I was unsure why she wanted to get together. Since the break up had been amicable (well, amicable enough), I allowed my imagination to run a bit wild.

We choose a restaurant located in the Yonge and Steeles area. As the server (an older woman) took us to our seats, I was preoccupied with my date: she was dressed well, and no new rings on her fingers (it's a drag if an ex has found The One while you're still looking). I was so preoccupied that I didn't notice it was taking quite a while to get to those seats.

When the server left, my ex-flame was irate.

"She put us at the back of the restaurant!"

Now I was jolted back to reality. By the way, did I mention my ex-flame was black? Once upon a time, I didn't think that detail would matter. She continued.

"When I worked as a server during university, I was always told to seat blacks in the back, so potential white customers wouldn't be scared off."

At this point, my mind was reeling. I wasn't naive enough to think racism didn't exist in Toronto, but putting blacks in the back? Was this Mississippi in the 1950s? I figured it was time to leave, but my ex-flame got up and led me to the front of the restaurant, where there were plenty of empty tables.

A young white woman came over to serve us, and my dining companion proceeded to carry on as if nothing had happened. I wish I could say the same. I followed her example, but it gnawed at me that a restaurant which was part of a well-known chain could allow this to happen in the 21st Century, especially in a city where racism doesn't exist.

My co-worker didn't have anything to say about this. And I never did find out why my ex-flame wanted to do lunch.

Notes

[1] Dudley Laws (May 7, 1934 - March 24, 2011) was a well known Canadian civil rights activist. He was born in Jamaica and came to Canada in 1965. Mr. Laws co-founded the Black Action Defence Committee in 1988.

[2] Herman Cain was a candidate for 2012 Republican presidential nomination.

[3] The Oakdale Community Centre is located at 350 Grandravine Drive.

My Story - Two (Male)

"It's only when you get involved yourself that you see things that are real."

I was born in Germany and I came over when I was twenty-one. I came because in Germany I had to go into the army and Canada had a volunteer army, so I escaped being a soldier.

Computers took away my livelihood. I was trained as a bookbinder, and I've been binding books since I was fourteen. That was fifty-eight years ago. I still bind books for people. I retired at sixty-two because it was very hard work. My main job at the plant was feeding the machine and taking out the folded paper. I'd move six tons of paper every day.

It was difficult when I first got here. There was one year where I changed companies six times. My English was not very good back then, and they were looking for experience, guys who had worked in the industry. I had knowledge of paper, but not the Canadian system of measurement. The weight of the paper was also different here.

After all my years here, I still don't know how they came up with the measurement for the weight of the paper. Five hundred sheets weigh so much and that's how they calculate it. In the bindery, I knew the difference between paper just like that. There were only four kinds of printing when I went to printing school. There are so many different kinds of printing processes nowadays.

Anything that deals with paper was considered book binding. That includes gathering and inserting sheets, cutting business cards, making glue, and so on. Speaking of glue, I learned how to make many kinds of glue, except for the synthetic glues which are the most common now. Those glues are patented.

I moved into the Jane-Finch area in the mid-1960s when my company moved up to Chesswood Drive (Sheppard Avenue West, south of Allen Road). They stayed there for about ten years. They used to be located down town at Adelaide Street near John Street until they sold that property.

This came at a time when the printing industry changed from letterpress to offset printing. With the excess money our company made from the sale, we bought new presses. We took four of the letterpresses with us to the new location, and when the use of lead ended, we used those presses to make pizza cartons. We had to convert them to cardboard presses from paper - someone managed to do that.

I ended up working at University of Toronto Press where they hired me as a cutter and eventually I worked up to a folding operator because I was so good on the folder. I worked there for ten years. Before that, I worked twenty-eight years at Garden City Press.

When Garden City Press moved to Mississauga, the company ended up sold to a judge in Winnipeg. We learned that this judge had six printing plants like ours all over Canada. He had to close one for some management reason. He played with us, by trying to reduce our wages and squeezing the union.

This happened around 1990. I was shop steward negotiating for the union with management about wages. I did calculations and I said to myself that this didn't make sense - even if I worked for nothing it wouldn't save the company if they were going downhill. Wages usually make up five to seven percent of every dollar that they charge, and they had to make fifty percent mark up. The pressmen conceded a fifteen percent wage reduction and vacation reduction. If you were there twenty five years, you got an extra week vacation. The pressmen gave that up.

Years later, I was sitting at a negotiation table for University Press with the same guy who allowed the union at Garden City to give up the fifteen percent. He said to me, "I got one more year out of them." Well okay, that's one way of looking at it.

What they did with me is ship my machine to a non-union shop. Since it was such a complicated machine, they wanted me to go there and show them how to run it. I said there was no way I could do that. No one there could run the machine - they wrecked it. You have to be sensitive with delicate machines. I knew it had to be oiled monthly.

Also, I cleaned under the machine so I could see if ball bearings or other parts were falling out. They didn't do any of that. There were so many small things on that machine that they goofed up.

Eventually, the machine was taken out of that non-union shop and stored in a trailer parked on our lot. I figure a salesperson over-estimated the capacity of that machine. Management never came down to see us on the floor. They said I wasn't fast enough, but they had no idea how complicated it was to run that machine.

There were no visible minorities in our area when I moved into Jane-Finch. I took in a coloured boarder and neighbours called the police on me. That was something. I gave him a key so he could get in anytime he came home. One day he came home and he was in no hurry to get in.

He fumbled around a little bit, then the neighbours saw that he was coloured and they called the police.

The way he told me the story when I got home, the police were not very nice. They asked him all kinds of questions so he had to show them proof that he lived there. He had the key, and he showed them his room where he had his stuff in the closet.

The police went through the house with their wet boots, leaving marks wherever they walked. I could see where they had gone. Later on, I went to the police station to talk about it. The station was located at Sheppard Avenue West back then, just east of Jane Street. I was told at the desk that they didn't know anything about it.

I moved into my house in 1967, but didn't get married until 1980. I used to rent out rooms. I had some long term tenants who were with me for fifteen years. One guy, Horatio was his name, he stayed a long time, even after I got married. I didn't need the room, so I didn't see why I had to ask him to leave. My wife didn't like it. Eventually he left. So when things go wrong in the house, we say, "Horatio did it." Whatever he did, he was allowed to do until I got married. After I got married, my wife didn't like what he did.

I put all my savings into mortgages back then. I had a lawyer who was feeding me mortgages, and that's how I was making money. An interesting aspect of our neighbourhood came out during the dealings I had with banks who were offering mortgages.

I paid my house off, so I was able to borrow money off the house. I went to the bank because I had to borrow $80,000. I usually went through the credit union, but I wanted to compare with another corporation that was offering mortgages.

The first thing they asked was the location of my property. I was in an area with single houses, and the man said, "If your property is in the southeast corner of Jane-Finch, we don't give mortgages." Had I lived in that area, I wouldn't have got a mortgage. There weren't a lot of streets in that southeast section back then, as there was a golf course.[1]

This was in the Seventies. I don't remember which company that was, but I remembered it in my head that nobody wanted to place a mortgage there. None of my mortgages were around this area. I went slowly out of the mortgage business after I got married.

It's been more than twenty years since I've held any mortgages. They weren't all good deals. I ended up with one property in Brampton that was $450,000, but today is only worth $360,000. I used to rent it out and I found people would wreck it more than it cost to maintain it. They'd wreck it and when you took them to court, you'd find tenants have the rights and they've got the power.

As a landlord, you've got no power. You never win, because you can't collect even if you've got a piece of paper saying you can. There's no sense taking them to court. Lots of people know that - tenants who've been through it before and know that the landlord can't collect, so they rent somewhere else. Lawyer's fees alone sometimes cost more than what you're trying to collect.

There are all different houses on my street. There is only one other house like mine. The lots are all about the same size, but most of them are not square. People think Jane-Finch is all highrises, but it's not.

My house's lot is fifty feet front by one hundred and fifty feet. There are lots of trees in the backyard. Where the houses were built, it must have been a forest previously.

I've got a very old oak tree in the backyard, but all the other trees have been removed since I moved in, and new ones have grown. I have basswood, ash, two beechnut trees, locust trees - they're slow growth hardwood trees which the city planted in front of my house. My son planted a flowering locust tree in the backyard. That's a fast growing tree, with many flowers and long branches.

When there's a storm, many branches break off, especially during heavy snowstorms. I've got evergreen trees, one in front of the house that the previous owner planted. I cut all the lower branches and park my car under it. So the sap from the tree covers my car. It does no harm. When the sap dries, I scrape it off. My visitors don't want to park under that tree, so I park there.

It's only when you get involved yourself that you see things that are real. Now with the issue of Jane-Finch being a bad neighbourhood, I was working too hard to really notice anything when I moved into the neighbourhood, but gradually I learned that this is a caring community. You learn this when you see one incident after another where you see someone taking care of somebody else who's in a little trouble.

I got involved in the community because I like to live here. I find a lot of nice people. The more I get involved, the more nice people I find. We always say don't talk to strangers, but when I talk to them, they're not strangers any longer.

I have seldom found a "real" Canadian who was born here. Most of the people in our community have come from somewhere else. Many of the elderly are ready to share their life stories. Most of the time, once I get them going, I just listen.

My main cause was our community hospital when we learned in 2006 that a new hospital was going to be built in a different location. I can say this cause was what got me involved locally. My neighbour alerted me on that. He told me that the Humber River Health Coalition was having a meeting. I went and there was about twenty-one people there fighting for the hospital. Some of them were going around collecting signatures for a petition. The petition asked to have some input on the decision where to put the new hospital.

Gradually, people gave up on the issue as being an impossible cause because the politicians ignored us. That's what I believe. We went to Queen's Park, we had nine thousand signatures, and we presented the petition to our MPP. They're adamant that the new hospital will be better and will serve the community better.

I don't believe what they are telling us when they say they've got public consultation, because at the last meeting we had with the CEO of the hospital, there were just five people present from the community. I asked if they actually do have public consultation - I didn't want to be cynical - and they said they did. I don't know how they publicized that event, as I was told about it by a person who attended, and I told my neighbour, who otherwise would not have known.

I don't use a computer; I read the paper, I go to meetings, and that's how I learn about things. I still go around collecting signatures every now and then. The wording has changed. Now we ask that our Jane-Finch hospital will serve the community in the same way as the new hospital once it is built. We don't want any part of hospital privatization. The government can borrow money cheaper than any private company.

They will sign contracts that the public never gets to see. These guys know everything ahead of time. Same with the new hospital at Wilson and Keele. A councillor told me that the decision to build at that location was made in 1999. That was seven years before we learned about it in this community.[2]

And coincidental with that, the people who bought property in the development beside the old Canadian Tire (Keele Street near Wilson Avenue) were told by real estate agents they were getting a good buy because there would be a hospital built down the road. I don't know the date that was announced, but it was definitely well before the Jane-Finch community knew about it. They used that as a sales ploy to lure people into buying.

Look at what happened to the piece of land located directly across from Yorkgate Mall.[3] We had a good idea how to develop that lot using the hospital as a hub. The funny part is when I asked at one meeting, four years ago (2009), why they don't expand the current building the extra three floors to make it ten storeys? When the hospital was first built, it was set up for future expansion. The CEO answered they were afraid of an earthquake. One hundred and twenty people were there, and they all laughed.

When I talk to the local students about the hospital, about eighty-five percent of them were born there. They say, "We don't want the hospital to go." I'll walk on the sidewalk in front of Westview Centennial Secondary School and I'll talk to the kids.⁴ I've been doing that for eight years now.

The local school (Gosford Public School) is quite small, but it sits on a huge chunk of land.⁵ Developers would love to get their hands on some of this land. It's not right that the school board wants to sell off any of this land, because these schools were built for the future. Now they're cutting the future off, saying they need money. They run the debt that way, so they have to sell these properties. I disagree with that because the future is that there will be more kids.

Right now, it's a temporary downslide. There are small houses on Gosford, across the street from the school. One day, they'll be torn down and highrises will be built there. Those houses were built with cheap materials and are not going to last. The property values on that land will go sky high and the taxes on each house will make it expensive to live there. Many of those units are single owners, but there are people who own more than one unit. One person owns over forty of them.

What has changed on my street is that different nationalities, other than Italian, have moved in. When I moved in, it was either Italians or immigrants like me from western Europe. It was relatively quiet. Lately, people have moved in who love their music. They probably lived in a highrise and the freedom of a backyard makes them inundate the neighbourhood with their music. That is unacceptable in my opinion. I go talk to them and I've been effective.

Italians buy houses like these, make them beautiful with nice front yard, they plant trees, and then they move out. I've heard that some people have moved out and later come back to the area.

Before I got involved in community groups, I did not know much about the other parts of Jane-Finch other than mortgages not being available. I certainly know better now.

Notes

¹ A large portion of the property owned by Northwood Golf and Country Club was developed by 1981.

² An official announcement about the new hospital was printed in this article: "Keele and Wilson home to new Humber River Regional Hospital," *Etobicoke Guardian*, 4 September 2007.

[3] Currently, that parcel of land remains empty. There was a report a few years ago that it would be used to build a TTC hub to service a planned LRT transit line running along Finch Avenue West.

[4] Westview Centennial Secondary School is located on the south side of Oakdale Road directly across from the hospital.

[5] The most recent enrolment figures for Gosford Public School (Grades JK to Six) shows 232 students.

Youth and Violence

Two of the biggest concerns in the community - why are they so often linked together?

I'm not optimistic about the future for our youth.

Why is it that as soon as shots are fired a mother's heart skips a beat? Because we realize we are now living in a world where you don't have to be a bad guy to get killed, and you don't have to be a drug dealer to be killed. Now you can be that youth coming home from school, from work, or even a friend's house. You can be sitting in your own yard and someone will come up to your son and take his life just to have the bragging rights of being in a gang.

So I get why our hearts skip a beat, because we are living in a time where a gunman will walk up to your front door in broad daylight and take your son's life. It is a mother's worst nightmare.

There's a new generation of kids here now. Things have calmed down. The older generation, the ones before them, they were more gun happy - most of those guys have passed away or are in prison. They were reckless. They really didn't care too much.

They were following the New York or Brooklyn or whatever kind of life style, the bad areas from the American projects. The ones on TV with their guns and their bling-bling - they wanted that image to make them look cool. All that unnecessary stuff because they weren't too educated.

This new generation is mostly about the guys making money - it doesn't matter if it's legal or illegal. When I say illegal, I mean either selling drugs or getting stuff from somewhere else and selling that merchandise - more like businesspeople, only they're selling the wrong product. It's harder to get a gun nowadays. Now that things have tightened up in terms of awareness, I think that it has calmed things down a bit. There are more eyes on people.

You have these kids growing up without fathers, and that cycle just keeps happening. They're having issues psychologically. Sometimes you

42

need a mother and a father to raise these kids. In a lot of these relationships, the father is absent - it does a lot of things to these kids. Then they let the streets start to raise them, to do the things that a mother can't do. Because there are a bunch of men on the streets. If you end up on the streets, you're going to find yourself ending up in some kind of trouble. You're going to get pulled over for something. Because of survival, you'll probably be holding something that doesn't belong to you.

And you have the young girls growing up without fathers, too. And I wonder if they see this as okay because you end up with a lot of young mothers having kids with young men who are not there, that don't know how to be responsible yet, they don't know how to be a father yet. So you're having young women having kids and that cycle continues. How do you stop it?

When I hear these stories of men from single family households who resort to crime, and people try to give reasons for that, it always makes me angry. If anything, you should be motivated to become a better person and get your mother and get yourself out of that situation. You don't resort to crime, or at least, I never resorted to crime. One of my best friends also comes from a single parent family. He happens to be black and he didn't resort to crime either. That's something that I think too many people use as an excuse.

It's funny: I'm very progressive but when it comes to crime, I don't want to say I'm conservative or right wing, but while I recognize there are systemic issues to crime, I don't like the excuse that someone came from a single parent household. It does an injustice to all youth who grew up in a one parent household.

The same goes for children who see a parent being abused. I saw my mother abused by my dad for a bit, and I'm not going to grow up and hit women. That's the thing I don't understand - if you saw your mother hit, you're going to grow up and hit your wife. I internalized it, I saw it, and thought why would I ever want to cause a woman that kind of pain? I just won't do that. There are a lot of excuses being made and I think people need to take ownership for their actions.

◆

It's like the guys wearing the hoodies and the big baggy pants, it's not because they want to do criminal activities or be drug dealers, it's just that's the style and the fashion that the media portray of what Jane and Finch is supposed to look like. If you don't look like that, you're not tough. If you're not tough, you're nobody.

◆

Violence can happen anywhere. And being here you know that if you don't have a problem with anybody, if you don't go out there making trouble, then nobody really bothers you. If you go out there searching for trouble, then trouble finds you. You're relatively safe living here in the community. Any place you go, you can be in the wrong place at the wrong time. The image they have of Jane-Finch where you can't go out at night or you'll be robbed - it's not really true.

◆

Here's one reason why you have a higher crime rate in our area: people take the law into their own hands because they don't feel protected by the lawmakers.

◆

One thing that we see now is that the federal Conservatives are replicating the strategy of the Harris Conservatives,[1] exaggerating crime and basically fear-mongering, even though statistics say crime is going down. They're pushing a zero tolerance on crime agenda when it's not needed. The reason they're doing it is to create a political wedge where they can get their share of voters, knowing this is an agenda the other parties won't follow.

It affects lower income communities like Jane-Finch, where we're seeing an increased police presence, and the increased harassment towards youth.

◆

From a community standpoint, safety is an issue as the youth of the coming generation have grown to be rootless, disconnected, and demoralized. They are almost like robots or characters in a video game! It's like their mind is being controlled by a remote and it is switched to the "divide and conquer" or "hate and war" setting, yet they have no clue what they're fighting against one another for.

It's like a pre-programming or preconditioning, especially where the youths are being raised in and under government housing.

◆

A lot of parents don't have a lot of time because they're working three or four jobs, so they're not able to be there for their children at a level where they need to be. The kids are out on the streets and the streets are raising them. It's not that the parents don't want to be there, it's that they need to be able to survive and feed their families.

The schools feel the burden because they're with the students from 9:00 a.m. to 3:00 p.m. The kids will come there without the nutrients they need, didn't have breakfast, so they can't focus and the classrooms are of a large capacity - there will be one teacher and maybe thirty students.

44

The cutbacks we've had in the schools doesn't allow for teachers' aides and support for the teacher. It's like the families need support, and they hope that the schools will be able to give support, but the schools have a heavy load themselves, so they're hoping to get some support too.

But we don't have the funding; in our area specifically, we've been cut back tremendously. This lack of support reflects in things like violence. While the parents are at work, trying to work those three or four jobs, there's nobody to supervise the children, and they're hanging out with bad crowds and picking up a lot of things that will cause them trouble.

This leads to things like the turf wars. For example, we have Dune Grassway on the west side of Jane and they do things in a specific way different from the east side of Jane Street. They have street codes (that's what they would call it) and wear different colours. A lot of the violence in Jane-Finch centres around youth.

This is what the youth do in their idle time, when they're on the streets hanging around. A lot of them have grown up in poverty and so they feel like they have to go out and survive somehow. You'll have the young boys on one end and they'll see some youth from the other end, and they'll want to take his shoes or his phone, rob him for his money.

That's their form of survival, that's their way of gaining stripes for their area. They're across the street from each other, with their own colours, and if they cross the street, it's very possible that someone could lose their life. And this is in a community that's supposed to be united in one way or another. That's what the youth have grown to know.

◆

From the beginning, before they started school, I spoke to my kids about religion, about culture, about respect, about education. I didn't just feed them with food, I fed them with words. I tell them to know what's right. They didn't have a father, but I think I raised them well. My son still tells me where he is going when he goes out.

When my son didn't respect his teacher, I made him go one week without watching TV or using the computer. Where I come from, what I believe, the teacher is like a mother. My son spends part of the day with me, he spends the other part with the teacher, and he has to respect her like me, like the mother and the father. Even if the father doesn't live with the kids, still they have to respect him too. They have to respect adults.

◆

I have three children, ages from seventeen to twenty-five. Two children are here in Canada, one lives in the States. I believe my children are better off being raised here. They were born here. So far they are good kids, they've never caused any trouble.

One of my sons wants to be an animator, he's a good artist who always gets very high marks in drawing. The art teacher at high school said it would be a good idea for him to get into animation. At his elementary school, they still display his art all over the school. He'll go to Humber College for art. There are many students taking that animation course. It's a three year course, the books alone are $500, each semester is $850. The government won't give any money for this course. My son thinks that when he's finished the course, he's heading to Hollywood to work in animation. That's all he ever wanted.

◆

The mentality of young men in this neighbourhood is terrible. They need help and they need it fast because their mentality is staying the same as they're getting older. Their outlook on life is not good. It is destructive, which would make Jane and Finch more destructive than it already is for the next generation to come.

◆

My dreams and aspirations for my children are for them to be successful and happy like every mother dreams for their children. I was never the one to dream big until I had my children come into my life. Then I dreamed big every single day when I woke up in the morning.

The main thing I want is for my children to be scared of our God, knowing the consequences will be severe in doing something against the religion. They know what to do and not do and what I hope is that they stick with that mentality for the rest of their lives.

◆

Don't put money in your child's hand because you don't know where they're going to go. I didn't give my son any money when he was young. When he asked me for money to go to McDonald's, I went with him there. When he asked for money for school lunches, I would phone the school and ask them if they were having a lunch, and how much?

I didn't do this because I was cheap, I was worried about my child. I wanted to be sure he didn't buy drugs or cigarettes. I didn't put the money in his hand until he grew up.

◆

My son called 911 while I was sleeping. He told the person that the house was on fire. I woke up when I heard knocking on the door. There were four police officers standing outside. My son was only three. When I needed to discipline them, I used time outs for my children. I would take away things that they liked.

◆

I came to Canada from my home in Cairo, Egypt. Living in Canada for most of my life it would be me either getting verbally abused or physically abused. That stuff never happened to me in Egypt. I've learned that living in Canada has its benefits and it has its negatives.

For some reason a bunch of girls my age decided to abuse me physically non-stop. At one point I was defenceless against two girls. I don't like to fight; to be honest, I don't fight, period. My face and body were bruised and swollen. It was the worst pain that I've ever experienced in my entire life. The reason for this physical conflict was due to the girls being jealous of my beauty and how I get more attention from the males than they do.

I didn't understand why they wanted to beat me over something like that. I didn't even know these girls and they just came up to me and punched me in my face and body. I didn't deserve the beating I got from these girls.

After that conflict happened, the police got involved and they did get charged for their actions against me. This will always scar both me and my family for the rest of my life.

◆

A lot of parents won't call the police because they're afraid Children's Aid will come and take away their kids.

The local youth can be role models by living here and working here. A lot of the single mothers here are role models for their children. They have to be mother and father to their kids, and they work so hard to look after them.

Over the years, the media have really done a number on single mothers in this neighbourhood. They blame single mothers for every bad thing that happens here, and that's not right.

◆

Youth in Toronto have too much access to guns, considering there are no gun stores in Canada and the youth don't know how to make guns. So it becomes a police issue because how are the guns getting in the city and what steps are they taking to prevent it?

The authorities are taking aggressive and competitive steps that are not healthy or a solution. Instead, it only aggravates the situation and causes the youth to become more brutal and senseless with their actions.

They need to make the youths feel valuable and useful. They need to give youth a way out instead of forcing them deeper into a life style that's not healthy for anyone, because their actions affect everyone, and just like in any game the object is to win and if we can show the youth how to win in life for good and not bad, more people would be happy and not sad.

◆

Whenever I read about a shooting that involves a teenager, my first reaction is sorrow. My second reaction is that we need to get guns out of hands. I believe it is already too late to make a noticeable reduction in the number of guns out there - with the way our friends south of the border have gone gun crazy and super-saturated their nation in lethal weapons, there's no way that genie gets put back into the bottle.

Somehow, we need to scare our young hands away from guns, to make guns as unattractive as possible.

I suggest that the justice system imposes a three year minimum sentence on every case of gun possession for anyone under whatever age we determine fitting.

No excuses, no exemptions, if you're caught with a gun on your person, you're gone for three years. Sorry that you made a bad choice, and now you need to pay for it. Make it clear that there are no excuses, no second chances, no minimum age limits (within reason). If you're old enough to carry a gun, you're old enough to be gone. Three years that you will be away from your family, your friends, and your freedom to do whatever you want.

Now, the key part of my suggestion is the purpose behind the time away. The only way I suggest such a sentence is that the convicted are required to spend the time either completing their education (high school diploma at the minimum) or learning a trade. They must not be rotting away day and night in a detention centre, counting down the time until they return to the streets, and picking up bad habits in the meantime.

Instead, they need to be applying themselves, working on something concrete, so that when the sentence is over, they come out with prospects for a productive life. It could be as simple as going to a regular school during the day, and spending the nights and weekends at a group home, shelter, or some other institution.

Discipline is key - homework must be done, the youth must behave at school, and made to pitch in for chores. Failure to do so means that the sentence is extended. Complete the sentence as required, and nothing goes on your record.

I believe that the vast majority of youth who carry guns are not lost causes. As I said earlier, wrong choices were made, and so society should offer these youths an opportunity to learn from their mistakes.

This is a short term solution. Its goal is to get guns and the people holding them out of the community right away. It's important that this is applied equally, regardless of race, area code, or connections. Once again I stress that it must give the option of getting an education or marketable skill, so that these youth return to their communities ready and able to lead more productive lives. The long term solution will take a lot more studying, planning, and resources to cure whatever social ills make our youths carry guns in the first place.

48

I remember a few years ago when I was talking with a woman who had relatives living in Harlem. She said they thought Jane-Finch was just as bad. That stunned me. People in Harlem, South Central L.A., the rough parts of Brooklyn - they think we're on the same level as them? Jane-Finch is the same as South Compton? Those places have more shootings in one month that the entire City of Toronto will have in two years.2 People across Canada think Jane-Finch is just so dangerous.

◆

A future for the children in Jane-Finch? I hope there will be more opportunities than we have right now. I hope there will be useful programs for kids and youths, particularly more skill enhancing programs to keep them active and engaged in the community so they don't stray and end up doing things that are negative.

◆

If we're looking for long term answers to the issue of youth violence, I think we need to demand more from our schools. Because children spend so much time at school, that's where they can build their self-esteem, nurture their skills, develop their minds.

The school has a child for six or seven hours a day, ten months a year, and that's a big chunk of time that can be used to counteract negative influences. A little more focus on critical thinking, so children not only learn to question but so they can make important decisions on their own. If schools can provide that, then they can demand parents and care givers follow through on their end. Make sure the children go to school, do their homework, spend a little less time on distractions.

This should be part of the curriculum in every school, not just something put in place for "priority areas." Children can slip through the cracks anywhere, and teachers should be trained so they can teach any students in any area.

When there are shootings involving youth, usually it turns out that the youth involved aren't going to school regularly, if at all. The system needs to reach out and make all students feel like they can fit in, learn something, become something. People wonder how youths can shoot at each other, and wonder why there is so little respect for human life. It's hard to respect others if you don't even respect yourself.

◆

I've known many people who've been arrested for shooting people or were themselves shot, whether they were classmates or acquaintances when I grew up. You become desensitized to it.

I remember the few times when it did hit me. The first was a guy who lived in my building. It was him and someone else who I went to school with. We were both in the same grade. They got arrested for killing somebody who worked at a car dealership. He was trying to repossess a car and they shot and killed him. That really affected me because I had seen them both just a couple of days earlier and now I saw them being wanted on the news.

The second was when Jordan Manners was shot.[3] His aunt was our neighbour, so I used to see him all the time. One boy who was arrested for shooting him was someone I used to see at school when I was younger, because I'm a couple of years older than them. I used to walk him to school. So I was thinking, "He really did that?" It really hits you. Other than those two, I've been really desensitized to it. Which is really weird because you shouldn't be.

Notes

[1] Mike Harris, leader of the Ontario Progressive Conservatives, was the 22nd Premier of Ontario from June 26, 1995 to April 14, 2002.

[2] "Those places have more shootings in one month that the entire City of Toronto will have in two years." This may be an exaggeration, though it's hard to be sure. The Toronto Police keep detailed statistics which are available to anyone (http://www.torontopolice.on.ca/statistics/ytd_stats.php). Here are the total number of shootings in Toronto over a recent three year period:
2010: 335
2011: 281
2012: 289

There doesn't seem to be any free source for statistics on shootings in any of the U.S. neighbourhoods mentioned. If we look at homicides, Jane-Finch doesn't seem quite so deadly. The city-wide total is in brackets:
2010: 3 (63)
2011: 3 (50)
2012: 2 (54)

In comparison, L.A.'s Compton neighbourhood recorded twenty-two homicides in 2012, while East Compton had seven. However, East Compton had zero homicides in 2011. That year, Watts was the most deadly L.A. neighbourhood with twenty-three homicides. It may be more instructive to look at the overall homicide totals for L.A. over the same period:
2010: 693
2011: 647
2012: 659

All Los Angeles numbers came from the L.A. Times web site (http://homicide.latimes.com/year/all). These numbers are more than ten times greater than the homicides in Toronto, yet L.A. (2012 population: 3.858 million is not ten times larger than Toronto (2012 population: 2.791 million).

[3] Fifteen year old Jordan Manners died of a gunshot wound inside C. W. Jefferys Collegiate Institute on May 23, 2007. He was the first person to be killed in a Toronto school. Police arrested two suspects after a series of raids. Because of their age, their identities were not made public. They were charged with first degree murder, but were eventually acquitted. The defense lawyers suggested Manners died when a gun went off accidentally in one of the school's washrooms. (Peter Small, "Two acquitted in Jordan Manners shooting," *Toronto Star*, May 19, 2011)

My Story - Three (Female)

"I'm actually surprised that I didn't turn out worse than I could have."

I guess I've had my moments of fame. The first time I was mentioned in the newspaper was for track and field. I came to Canada when I was ten, and shortly after that I ended up in the care of the Catholic Children's Aid Society. I was being moved all over the place through foster group homes and I think that was because the first home the Society placed me in was not black.

So I felt awkward, coming from a country where I saw hardly any white people and now I'm the only black person in this home. The food was very different - Jamaican food was what I was used to and now I'm looking at weird stuff. Just as an example, I thought mashed potatoes were weird.

I found myself eating a lot of cereal for breakfast, cereal for lunch, bread and cheese. The food was disgusting, and maybe that was because the person didn't know how to cook. I've had a lot of Canadian food since then, and the food tastes fine. In addition, this woman had a dog that shed a lot of hair. There were times I'd find hair in the food and that was a big turn off. I complained my way out of that home.

I went to a home with a Jamaican family. They were both correctional officers and they ran the place like a jail, literally. I remember getting into a fight there one time. I was the youngest one there at the time and this older girl always picked on me. It got to the point where I just fully attacked her.

That was the first time I was restrained. I felt like I couldn't move, like I couldn't breathe, just by the way they held me and that was something they used from their training as correctional officers.

I also went through a lot of middle schools, and the last place I ended up in was the Parkdale area. I started Grade Nine at Parkdale Collegiate. Back in Jamaica, I did a lot of running. Not for school though; I ran because I was always in trouble. At Parkdale, I got into track and field because I enjoyed the sport.

Merlene Ottey was one of the big track and field stars in Jamaica. My goal was to get to the Olympics and be like her. I did really well at it. My coach said that the level I was at in Grade Nine was comparable to the level of someone in Grade Eleven.

I made it to the finals my first year. I screwed up in the finals, but I was one of the first Grade Nines my coach had ever seen to make it to the finals. During the semi-finals, the Toronto Daily Star came and took photographs. I remember when I saw the article, because when I was running in the semi-finals, my team mates were telling me, "Did you see how far ahead you were of all the others?"

I couldn't comprehend it until I saw the photograph and the distance that I was ahead of the other competitors.

And that was the first time I entered the news. The second time that I know about is an article with me discussing Children's Aid where they talk about my accomplishments growing up in the system and what I've accomplished so far.

There's also a newspaper story about my involvement with Women Moving Forward (WMF). I got into WMF because I had a friend, Talia,[1] who was doing her school placement at the Jane/Finch Community and Family Centre (JFCFC).

Initially, she didn't want to do the placement there, but I told her if you get hungry, you can come upstairs to my place. (Note: JFCFC has offices located on the ground floor of a few local residential apartment buildings. Women Moving Forward is a program offered by JFCFC).

Once Talia started the placement, she learned about WMF. She told me, "You know what? This is a great program!"

I was already at Emery Collegiate doing their upgrading program. I got pregnant in Grade Ten and dropped out of school. I was fifteen when I got pregnant. I had my daughter when I was sixteen, and I had my son when I was seventeen.

After I had my daughter, I went to school for one semester. Then I got pregnant again, and I went to Humewood House. That's a school for pregnant woman. It's also like a shelter setting for young single mothers to help you transition. There were far more complications with my son, so I stopped going to school. That's why I had to go to Emery for the upgrading program.

Because I was enrolled at Emery, I didn't want to go to WMF, but Talia said, "They give you food! They give you bus tickets! You get vouchers to go to the grocery store!"

Being a single mother, that clinched it for me. WMF had an age criteria and I was one year younger than it. I met with the program coordinator and she mentioned the age criteria and that I was too young.

True, but I told her I was more mature than my years. I was accepted into the two year program.

I found WMF was very helpful for me in terms of determining where I would go from there, because the program offered a lot of support. It really helped me figure out what I wanted to do, post-secondary, and it helped me upgrade my English.

I don't know if I was one of the top persons in the program, but I was the one who received the scholarship that was offered to one person completing the program.

There was a sisterhood there at WMF. There were a few problems between us at times, but it definitely brought the residents a lot closer. It helped me get into Humber College, helped with the application process, paid for the application fee, and the education component of WMF helped me pass the tests to register as a Mature Student. I definitely have a lot to thank them for in terms of getting to where I am now.

The staff at WMF were all great. I used to love the counselling sessions. We'd go and have a meeting, just talk about the issues that we faced as women. We were able to draw from each others' strength. At times where I felt like I was in my situation by myself, those circles helped me recover. It was definitely a great experience.

My mother had my sister when she was sixteen, my sister had her first child when she was fifteen, and I ended up in the same boat. It was the same thing with my aunt. When I told my mother that I was pregnant, I was more scared to tell my brother than her.

My brother was seven years older than me, and was my father figure. Because of the respect I had for him, I felt that I was really letting him down, so I told my mother to break the news to my brother.

When I told my mother, she wasn't getting all, "Oh no, why'd you get pregnant, I can't believe this happened!" Instead, the first thing she mentioned was track and field. The thing is that my mother never went to any of my track meets; instead it had been my brother who'd show up and take pictures.

I didn't grow up with my mother. She sponsored us to come here, and when we got here, she was very busy. We didn't see much of her, and she had this habit of disappearing for months.

So it was my brother, who was seventeen when we got here, who took on everything. That included combing my hair, which made me look crazy, by the way, because he didn't know how to comb hair, and all the kids would make fun of me. But he really tried his best.

The longest period my mother disappeared was six months. She went back to Jamaica around the time her mother passed away. But she was a landed immigrant. You can't leave the country for six consecutive months or else you default your permanent residency.

We thought that we were never going to see her again. The first time we felt that was when she left us in Jamaica because we didn't hear from her for a very long time. Now it was reversed, except that my sister, who was the eldest, was not there to support us. In Jamaica, it was all of us. Here it was just me and my brother. That was the first time Children's Aid got involved.

When my mother left, she was on social assistance. She gave my brother her debit card to pay the rent. When you're on social assistance, they send you assessment forms that you need to fill out. She wasn't there to fill out the forms, so they cut her off.

Now we had to go to a shelter, and that wasn't the first time, that was like the third or fourth time we had to go to a shelter. We had to go back to the shelter we just came from, Family Residence in Scarborough, on Kingston Road. It was the only place we knew where to get help, so we went there.

One of the staff called Children's Aid. At the time they thought it was best that my brother take care of me because he was of legal age. They helped him get on social assistance as a single parent. So he was seventeen on social assistance as a single parent to take care of me.

It was about a month after my mother came back that I actually went into care. She was hurting because her mother had passed away, and she took that out on me, physically and verbally. I was telling my friend at school to let her know what was going on - I didn't know she was talking to the principal.

One day I went home and a social worker was there waiting for me. She told me that my friend had told the principal what was going on at home and they thought that for my safety they needed to remove me from the house. I was eleven.

While I was in care, there were times I lost contact with my family because I didn't have the phone number. It was like we were all in our own spaces. My brother was in Hamilton, my mother was wherever she was, and I was wherever I was at the time. We lost contact for over a year.

One day I was in Scarborough, because that's where I stayed the most. I was living in the group home run by the correctional officers. The way they organized the place was they lived with their children, but you weren't really a part of the family. If they had their family functions or any outings, they'd tell the girls to go wherever. Of course, these girls were eighteen, seventeen, sixteen, so they had places to go. I was twelve. I didn't know anybody, I didn't have anywhere to go, so they got me a gym membership at the YMCA in Scarborough Town Centre. Whenever they had their places to go where they wouldn't take us, I'd go to the YMCA and stay until my curfew.

One day I was rollerblading in Scarborough and my brother was on the bus. He got off the bus and said, "What are you doing here?"

And that's how I resumed contact with my family. I got his number and from there, my mother's number. I made the effort to keep calling them and keep the connection with them.

For me, the experience in care was very lonely and isolating. I felt there really wasn't an effort to improve my experience and whatever I was going through. In a sense, I'm actually surprised that I didn't turn out worse than I could have. Just going through it, I understand why so many children in care end up in crime or they're doing drugs or something or the other.

When I look back at my experiences over the past sixteen years, I'd say there's been a lot of improvement. At one point, I'd never pictured myself being in this position.

When I had my daughter, for some reason I thought I'm going back to school, I'm going to get a proper job, I'm going to do everything. When I had my son two years later, I thought, okay, maybe I'll be one of those welfare moms. Instead, I've got two diplomas. I wouldn't say I have a career, but I've had a full-time job for the past three years. If it hadn't been for God, I don't think I'd be here.

My friend who did her placement at JFCFC got hired there when it was finished. Before she got hired, we did a lot of outreach. There were times we needed to put up flyers and we wanted to make any kind of extra money so we'd put up flyers for whatever amount we were given, and I pretty much got more involved with that.

She was doing her placement when the "Jane-Finch Is Getting On" forum was organized. Prior to that, she was always volunteering me for everything. It got to the point where I'd notice if she didn't ask me.

So I went to help out with the forum, and then I'd go to the meetings that followed, which led to me being a member of Jane-Finch On The Move. As I attended the meetings, I got to see the issues that affect the area. I thought that this is something I need to be involved in, especially since I live in the community. This was the same time I was in WMF.

I was the last born, and from what I know, I was the most spoiled of the four. My mother was very business-minded in Jamaica before she travelled. She'd go to places like Cayman Islands, and she'd buy and sell stuff. From what I recall, we had a really nice house compared to my other family members, located in the nicest part of the ghetto. It had a cement roof, not a zinc roof - I remember that much.

When she decided to leave, what I remember the most is that she decided not to leave me with my family. Instead, she left me with a person whose occupation was child care for rich families, travellers, tourists, or business people who brought their child with them. It was like another group home setting.

She left me and my brother at that place but because my sister was older, she was left with the house. At the time, my sister was fourteen and she had a house to herself - yes, we do a lot of stuff at a very young age down there! The children up here are spoiled. The responsibilities that we are given at such a young age (in Jamaica) - it's ridiculous.

I remember so clearly the day my mother actually left. I was used to her coming and going. It'd be goodbye and a lot of candies - there'd always be something in it for me. This time was different. Usually she'd just leave us with my sister, who was like a mother really. She didn't go to school. My mother told her to take care of your siblings, and that was it.

This time she brought my brother and me to a different place, telling me she'd be back in a month. She took us to a fast food restaurant and we were there eating the food. Later she was just talking to me, saying she'd be back in a month and crying. I asked why she was crying. She knew it wouldn't be a month. She was going somewhere and staying there.

The place where she had left me, initially, it was okay because my brother was there. It was a very strict home and my brother wasn't used to that. He ran away and went back to my family. After that, the place was very abusive. The woman running it was a Christian, quote unquote - yes, she went to church and read her bible. We used to wake up at five or six o'clock every day to pray.

She had a very lush house, almost like what you'd see in a Beverly Hills area. She was a teacher by profession, so we were home schooled. Say she had to go to the market or had to go out. There was three girls and two guys, one of them an older boy. She would strip us to our underwear so that we wouldn't leave the house. She would lock the door.

She had a nice backyard with a lot of mango trees and fruit trees, but we couldn't go there. We got used to it but it got to the point where this older boy, who was around sixteen, would be left in charge. When she left, he would put on porn movies, lock the other boy in his room, and he would molest the rest of us.

One day I said I would tell on him. He chased me into the bathroom, he pushed me into the bath tub, my forehead hit the faucet and all I remember seeing was blood all over my face. That cut needed seventeen stitches. I was five years old.

This is something else I remember her doing. She had an indoor washroom, and kind of a washroom on the outside. She didn't want us to use the bathroom. If we wanted to have a bowel movement, she would have us go on newspaper that she put on the floor. Then she'd throw that paper next door.

So when I got my forehead all busted up, the guy told the lie that I was trying to use the indoor washroom, and when he confronted me about it, I fell into the tub. So he didn't get into trouble. I did.

My mother was sending her money to take care of me, but I guess over time she faced financial difficulties because she stopped sending the money. As soon as the money stopped, the treatment got worse. I was getting a lot more beatings. I was always being reminded that I shouldn't be eating because my mother wasn't sending any money for food.

I don't know why she kept me there if she wasn't getting paid. Maybe she expected a lump sum, maybe my mother made promises, because I know they spoke on the phone every so often. When I asked my mother about it later on, she said she left a business back there, and other family members were supposed to pay that woman when my mother couldn't send the money.

I got hit in the head by a hammer with that lady. I started having nightmares and they were always about the day my mother left. I would be revisiting that day over and over. I would wake up crying. So one day, when she was waking me up to pray, I really jumped up because I was in the middle of a nightmare. And she hit me in the head with a hammer.

That woman kept telling me I had the mark of the demon on my forehead because of the scar I got from hitting the faucet. And I was treated as such. Then she would tell me both my sister and I had the mark of the demon. My sister also had a scar on her forehead, though not as big as mine. I don't remember how she got it. My sister never lived there, but once a month I could visit my family, and that's how she saw the mark on my sister's forehead.

I didn't tell my sister or any of my family what was going on. The way this woman was, if you were talking or misbehaving, she would pinch you really hard when no one was looking. It was one of those pinches where it looked like your skin was about to cut. So you would know not to say anything, and she was always there.

My mother also owned a boat. She had someone who would go fishing, sell the fish, and give my aunt the money. Only my aunt wasn't using the money as she was supposed to, which was to send my brother to school and pay for me at that home. I was still at that home three or four months after my mother stopped sending money.

Shortly after that, I ran away and went back to my family. My sister, my brother, and I were all back together in the house that my mother left my sister in. I spent most of my time with my grandmother because we all lived in the same neighbourhood. She made castor oil from scratch. Castor oil is good for your skin, good for your hair, and it's expensive. She had a client from England who had family in England and they would buy it, and she would make money that way.

My grandmother would also cook. She was pretty much what I would call a hustler. I was always around her, and she would get me into the beans and everything to help make the castor oil. I would always be fed if she was there. When she would visit her mother in the country, I would always go because that was farm country. They were growing yams, corn, cane, tangerine trees, and all other kinds of fruit. I liked to go there, because I knew whenever I was there, I would never be hungry.

In terms of taking care of us, my sister was now the primary person. At that time she had a child, and she was responsible for feeding us. She was sixteen at the time. She had her son when I was five.

My sister got a job when I was six or seven years old. My mother's house was all gated, so what my sister used to do was lock me and her son in the house because she couldn't find a baby sitter. The funny thing is that she would give me money to buy stuff but I couldn't leave the house because I was locked in without the key.

So I'd have to call out to people as they walked by, and give them the money through the window so they could buy something and put it through the window.

I wasn't in school and we weren't getting a lot of support from family members. They'd be saying, "Your mom's in Canada, what is she doing for you?" Nobody paid for my tuition.

There were bills, but we didn't pay them. If there were light bills to be paid, the government shuts off the lights. There'd be one or two persons who paid for light, so we'd run wires within the houses so we'd have light. We'd call it "stealing light." There was no mortgage because my mother built the house and everything was covered. As for food, my sister was working. Her boyfriend, her child's father, was also helping out.

There was a person I was told was my father. Apparently he had denied me up until the point where I looked like him. He didn't take ownership until he found out that my mother was in the process of sponsoring us for Canada. That's when he tried to be more involved, and give us money here and there. I guess he had it in mind that if he started now, when I went to Canada I would remember him. That's just how I view it. The first time I returned to Jamaica, he was just pure money hungry. I tried my best to avoid him, because he was all about money.

I went to school for one semester. Someone who knew my mother paid for that one semester. That was it for school. I had a friend whose parents couldn't afford to pay for his school either, so we hung around together a lot.

We would go down to the swamp, which had crocodiles, so it was dangerous. On his rooftop, he had this collection of different birds, because he would go into the trees and get the nests. People would buy them. He was eight at the time. We just hung around a lot.

At night time, me and my other cousin would go around to collect bottles in people's yards. We'd sneak into their yards so we could sell the bottles to a soft drink and beer company. We'd go to parties where people were drinking, just to collect the bottles. I was six years old - talk about maturing quick. By the time I came up to Canada, I had experienced so many things that it was somewhat difficult to relate to kids here. I found them to be immature.

I remember the first day I came into the shelter where we stayed, my accent was so thick, and for some reason I didn't understand what the word "English" meant. So I remember this girl was asking me "Do you speak English?" in Canadian English, and I said yes, but she asked again, so I said "No?"

I didn't know what the heck she was saying. At that time I thought, "What does that word English mean?" It's funny when I think back at this first interaction with this girl who was trying to make friends with me. There was that communication barrier, even though we did speak English. Also, I was so used to being in a black environment and here was a little white girl talking to me! It was more of a shock for me that she was talking to me, and maybe that's why I went blank. Not until I returned did I realize there were white Jamaican persons that I never saw as being white. It never dawned on me because of the accent. Afterwards, I started seeing the difference.

The first day we moved to Hamilton after the shelter, I remember this girl called me an alien. I didn't really comprehend what that meant. She said her parents told her I was an alien and I would be going back to my home. I thought she meant we were green Martians, so I got really angry and hit her for calling me an alien. I got suspended for that.

I remember that there was only one other coloured person in the school I was attending. He was Mexican. That was Grade Five. We were very close. There were a lot of Yugoslavians. I'd go into the Yugoslavian church. I would just walk in there and listen to them in their language. People would be looking at me. They'd pat my head and ask about my hair. For me, it was great because I was getting attention.

Eventually, we ended up moving. I got suspended twice. The second time I hit a guy with a badminton racket. My mother put braces on me and this guy was always making fun of my braces in gym class. The birdie hit me in my mouth, and I saw him laughing so I knew it was him. When he saw the look on my face, he started running. I threw the racket and it went straight to his head. He fell to the floor. When he got up, he was angry. At that time, I had a lot of rage, and I was ready to fight. The teacher had to split us up. We both got suspended.

From there, we moved back to Scarborough. That's when we moved into the house just before my mother went back to Jamaica for the six months. There was always a lot of moving around.

It wasn't until I was on my own that I lasted a full year in one place. I don't want my kids to go through this moving around and switching schools here and there. Now when I'm on the street, I'll see people I recognize from school and I'll try to figure out which one. "Was it Nelson Boylen? Parkdale? West Tech? Central Tech?" There were very few actual true friendships that developed because I was all over the place.

I have a diploma in Police Foundation. The reason I got that goes back to the group home where I stayed the longest. I went AWOL a lot. Every time I went AWOL, the police would get called because the home would have to report me missing, and when I came back, they'd have to call the police. The police would come, ID you, fill out their reports, give you some threatening gestures, and leave.

Once there was this black female officer who came. I had all this attitude, "Do your thing, fill out your report, and go," and she asked to speak to me in a separate room. She sat me down and said, "You know what? I have two daughters who are around your age and it breaks my heart to see you in this position. Right now I can tell you don't have any person for support and I would like to be that person."

She gave me her cell phone number, her home phone number, and her work phone number, to keep in touch with her. I didn't.

At that point, I believe I felt that she was faking because I had had so many Children's Aid workers pretend to make this connection with you and then they'd get a promotion or just leave. It got so I didn't want to get attached to anybody. The next time I saw this officer, I was in jail.

I found out my sister was really sick. At that time I was in a group home for females. When you had your period, they'd give you twenty dollars to buy female hygiene stuff. Plus you'd get a five dollar phone card to contact whoever you need to contact. This particular time, they didn't have any phone cards. When this happened before, they'd give you five dollars to buy the phone card. But this staff person was fairly new and she refused to give me the five dollars. So I got really upset because I didn't know what was going on with my sister.

At that first group home run by the correctional officers, I got restrained when I fought, so from then on I decided instead of being physical with someone, I would just break stuff. So because this staff person was blocking me, I went into the cabinet and I took out some of the best glasses.

I went into the backyard and started throwing them against the wall. She felt this was scary, so she locked the back door. The front door was still open. So I came back inside, I got some more glasses and began throwing them. That day I had track and field practice, so I just went there. At practice, I ran off a lot of frustration. When I came back, I was a lot calmer. It was grocery day, so my regular worker had been out, but now she got back there, too.

So I was in the basement helping to put away groceries. Suddenly there were these two huge police officers, and just the way they came in, with the macho attitude and being in my face, and going on about what I did and what I didn't do. So I said, "Hey get out of my face, you're not my father."

The next thing I knew, well actually, I still don't know exactly what transitioned. I was being flung against the counter, flung against the washing machine, and I was placed under arrest. I do remember that one officer kept asking if I was a citizen. When I said no, he said, "Well you know this can f*** up your chances of being a citizen, right?"

I didn't know what this had to do with anything. When I was in the back of the police car, I was just crying, and he was calling me names and laughing at me and my predicament.

The holding centre they brought me to was located at the station where that black female officer worked. I was in the holding cell, and decided that I was going to try my best to not be depressed. So I sang Bob Marley songs.

I saw her come by and I saw the look she gave me. She was so disappointed. She asked why I didn't call her. I didn't have a valid excuse. She asked what happened and I told her. She told me what the officer had said about me being landed and all that shouldn't have taken place.

I got charged with assaulting a police officer. What he called "assault" happened when he was holding his arm around my throat, and I was trying to pull it away. Somehow, he got a three centimetre scratch. This was like an awakening for me. I spent two days there, one day in the holding cell. It was almost the weekend, so the Children's Aid staff were trying to make sure I didn't spend the weekend there. They tried to get me to the court on Jarvis as soon as possible and get bail.

I remember the night they were bringing me to court. There were these girls from Regent Park in the same vehicle with me. They were talking, and it was like a joke for them being in the car and being transported to the court. They talked about how they fed up this girl, and I thought, "This is not for me."

After I got back to the group home, I was pretty good. My mother got back into the picture. She had opened a store selling ladies fashions in the Oakwood area.

Because she was travelling all the time to go to the States, she wanted me to be in charge of the store. That was me at fifteen. I had to put stuff on the mannequins, be the cashier, deposit the money in the bank, and all of that. It was supposed to be my brother's job, but he got attached to his pals in Hamilton, so it was me and my boyfriend instead.

Looking back, I wonder why my mother allowed us to have a relationship at that age. I can't see doing that with my daughter. A boyfriend at fourteen? Please! She was so open to it. Maybe because he was keeping me company in the store while she was gone.

There was one time when I thought it was wrong - keep in mind that I was running wild at the time and yet I still thought it was wrong - when the three of us went to the States. We were in the hotel, and there were two beds, a single and a queen bed. I'm already thinking it's going to be my mother and I in the queen, and my boyfriend by himself.

She puts me and him in the queen, and she takes the single bed! My boyfriend was nineteen at the time. They smoked their weed together and had a few drinks.

I don't smoke, so I was looking at them, and I couldn't believe this was happening. So he's high and drunk, and we're there sleeping, and he's trying to touch me.

"Are you serious? My mom is right there!" I guess because she was drinking and smoking with him, he felt that comfortable. So I'm there thinking that yeah, there's something wrong with my mom.

We were running the store and eventually there was an intervention from Children's Aid. They told me that I was a kid and I could not be in charge of a store. It didn't work like that in Canada. I wasn't going to let my mother's business fail because of them, so I left.

I went and stayed with my boyfriend for a good three weeks. The police were called. They said I was under age and by law, I had to be in school. It was either that or get arrested.

So I said I'd go back. Only it wasn't to the home where I was before, but another group home in Scarborough. That's where my boyfriend lived, so I thought that was good. Only I noticed over time he became abusive. It started verbally and then a bit of hitting here and there. So I thought maybe this was a relationship that I didn't need to be in. I told him over the phone that I was breaking up with him.

The next day when I was going to school, he was waiting at Warden station for me. He had a knife and he was saying, "I'm going to kill you, I'm going to kill myself, unless you take me back."

I was very scared but in order to calm him down, I didn't go to school that day. We went to the Dufferin Mall, because my school was in Parkdale. I was going to Parkdale because my track coach from Grade Nine was still there. He even paid for me to go to University of Toronto in the summer and train.

I was able to calm down my boyfriend, get the knife and throw it on top of the Dufferin Mall's roof. We were hanging around for the day, and when it got time for me to go back, it was a day where I had counselling. Apparently I was a depressed or disturbed child. Children's Aid had an assessment where I was shown images of splattered ink and based on what I said I saw, they thought I needed help. So I was going to group sessions with other Children's Aid kids, and this was one of those days. I just wanted to get back, because this group home was really strict.

We went to his place in Malvern, where I was anxious to leave for counselling, and he wanted me to stay. It got to the point where he was blocking the door. So I decided I was going out through the window. There was this back and forth, and he was pushing me. My clothes were ripped from all the pushing back and forth. I don't know how he hit me, but my mouth started bleeding. That's when he stopped, saying, "Look what you made me do."

His mother was knocking on the door because it was locked. She came in, saw me crying, and her question was, "Did you cheat on him?" Seriously?

I couldn't leave and take the bus because of how I looked, so I called the group home to come get me. When the worker arrived and saw the condition I was in, she took me to the hospital.

The police were called, they took a picture of my swollen lip and everything else. They also wanted to check if I had any fractures, so I underwent a pregnancy test to see if I could have x-rays.

The doctor came in and told me the pregnancy test came back positive. I looked at her, and once again, there was this look of pity, like, "I pity you right from the bottom of my heart."

I just laid down on the bed and covered my face with the sheet.

There was a restraining order on my baby's father. The police took my report, went to the Dufferin Mall, found the knife on the roof, and they charged him.

I thought, I'm pregnant, I don't believe in abortion, because that came up. My coach told me I was really young, I had a lot of potential athletically, which was good because my grades were lousy. I felt like all my coaches ganged up on me at Parkdale. I was also in basketball and volleyball, to stay active in the winter. So I left the school.

I also got kicked out of the group home because I was pregnant. Children's Aid had to get me into a shelter for women. That's where I met Talia - we were both pregnant and we were both loners.

I remember one Christmas, everybody went somewhere except for me and Talia. We really clicked there. The shelter was set up that you'd get an allowance, but you had to do chores. A lot of the girls there already had their support or someone giving them money. We'd split up their chores between us, and we'd have sixty dollars a week which we needed for baby clothes.

Eventually, I worked with Children's Aid to get the restraining order lifted on my child's father because I needed to have some kind of relationship if we were having a baby. They sent me to do anger management. The good thing about getting pregnant at an early age is that it took me off what could have been a destructive path. I had a temper, I was quick to fight, I was just mean, and I didn't care. When I found out I was pregnant, I told myself I couldn't do this any more.

What was driving me was the fear of having my child taken away. I wanted a family, I wanted to live on my own, all of that. Looking back on my transcripts, I can see my grades got much better. Back in Parkdale, my average was fifty, and I think some of the teachers bumped up my marks just so I could move on. There were classes at the shelter and my marks were seventy-eight, ninety-two, eighty. Even my two diplomas are both with honours.

The reason why I got into Police Foundation was because of that one interaction with the police officer. It was the thought of what could have happened had I taken her up on her offer. I wanted to do it, but I was too embarrassed to even call her.

I wanted a career where I could reach out to youth, especially those in my position. I wanted to be a police officer, so I could deal with people the way that officer tried to deal with me. I thought I could meet more high-risk youth working as an officer.

As I got along in the program, and I got more involved in the community, I questioned my decision. I saw that the youth have a negative relation with police officers. So if that barrier's already up, the youth aren't in a position where they want to hear you, they won't want to even see you. Instead, I went to community justice, where you're dealing with at risk youth involved with the justice system on a community level.

One time, Children's Aid thought that I needed a mentor, so they got me an older woman. She read my file. Then she looked at me and said,

"Most of the people that I mentor are into drugs or prostitution. How can you do this?"

To be honest, I don't know. I'm a strong-willed person and nothing can keep me down. I became the first one in my immediate family to have a high school diploma.

So I want to continue on this path so my daughter can look at me and see that even though I had situations that I could have used as excuses, I did not. I don't want her to end up in the position that I was in. I definitely don't want to be a thirty year old grandmother. I don't want my daughter to feel so isolated and so unloved that she feels only a guy can put that aside, when it's just infatuation.

Now I'm working at a bank, and I've been there almost three years. I work in customer service. I can give information on some products, like indirect loans. It doesn't tie in with my education.

While I was in school, there were two summers that I was on social assistance because I couldn't find a job. I was in a position where I needed to finish school, I needed a job, I needed to get off social assistance. So I got into security training. I was looking for a security job so I could get into my field.

I also filled out an application at the bank, and they gave me an interview just as I completed the training. I found out the bank was offering nearly sixteen dollars an hour to start, while I was looking at a security job for twelve dollars an hour. The dollars spoke more loudly at the time. I had to do my classes and placement on a part-time basis, and dragged it out for three years. In order to get into my field, I need more experience and that's an issue right now. The bank does have a lot of opportunities for growth. They have a security department, so I can move into that direction with my diplomas.

One day I'll have my house with a backyard. I have to have a cherry tree, no matter how long it takes to grow one. That's the plan. Have my children run around, though by that point, they may not want to run around. Maybe they'll have barbecues. My daughter's ten, my son is going on nine.

I feel so old, but I'm only twenty-six.

Notes

[1] "Talia" is an alias.

Education

"Teachers would call me lazy and an underachiever."

All my years of education were in this community. It was a big letdown - horrible schooling, horrible teachers. I didn't realize this until I got into university and interacted from kids from other schools and other areas. A friend and I were taking a course with three hundred other students. We weren't happy with the marks we got on a paper. We spoke to the professor who didn't know either of us or that we were friends. He asked if we went to the same high school. How did he know? It was because we had made the same fundamental errors in the writing style.

I have friends who went to teacher's college and they didn't want to do placements in the Jane-Finch area. More resources are put into schools outside the area.

Kids are sent out of school so that they can get their lives back on track. When I was in high school, I got a letter putting me on academic suspension. My mother fought it. The vice-principal put me on a contract where I had to send in bi-weekly reports.

I was the only student whose mother fought for them. There were two who ended up having run-ins with the law. This isn't universal for the Toronto District School Board (TDSB). I wasn't motivated prior to this, but now I was getting high marks. I'm not sure why I wasn't motivated before.

My Grade Eleven physics teacher once told me I should just drop out and save the taxpayers money. Another time, the counsellor came to the class to hand out application processing forms for universities. I was seated at the front. When she got to the back, she ran out of copies. So she came back and took the copy away from me, saying I wasn't going to need it.

A few years ago, I was asked to talk at a TDSB young men's leadership conference. This invitation came through my organization (where I work), not my old high school. There were a few youths from Jane-Finch at the conference. I didn't think they looked too impressed when I got up to speak. Once they heard I came from Jane-Finch, you could see them brighten up.

Teachers would call me lazy and an underachiever, yet no one ever looked into the issues I had with learning disabilities. Now doctors tell me it is a miracle that I progressed as far as I have with all these issues.

In Grade Twelve, I had to discuss terrorism for a presentation. I spoke about how America was doing things around the world. The teacher gave me a F, and said I was anti-Semitic. I was upset and went to the vice-principal. The department head read my presentation. He was Jewish and said there was nothing anti-Semitic about my presentation. He gave me an A. He ended up re-grading everything I did for that class and I got an A overall.

My feeling is that it was the older teachers who cared. I remember a teacher who helped me after class. One day, it was getting close to five, and I was still in the classroom with him. He called his wife to say he couldn't take their son to the eye doctor because he was still at school. That impressed me so much.

I want to be an engineer. It's pretty tough at Westview.[1] The teachers aren't bad, but the transition from middle school was difficult. Back in middle school, I was warned that in high school, the teachers wouldn't care if you walked out of the classroom.

I had a teacher who gave me a reality check, telling me I wouldn't go anywhere if I didn't take high school seriously. I didn't take him seriously, but Grade Nine was the toughest year for me. I passed all my courses. I didn't try to test the teachers and walk out, because my mother told me not to do that.

There are some teachers who care and others that don't. There were four or five kids like me who weren't doing well in math. The teacher would pick on us, asking why we were in academic.

I have a friend who's very athletic, who was also not doing well in math. He was the first person in Westview history to win Ontario Provincials. Every time there would be announcements enhancing him, the math teacher would denigrate him, try to put him down, telling him he wouldn't get anywhere without grades.

Day care would be a great start to altering the minds of young children susceptible to becoming a menace to society. Furthermore, elementary school is also the best time to explore the talents of these children, steering them in the right direction. As files are often carried with children as they graduate and change schools, the communication should stay open as well. When no one keeps track, a lot of our children fall through the cracks.

I remember when I was in elementary school, I had a great mind for poetry. I was appointed by my teacher and taken to C.W. Jefferys School of Arts in my young age and placed in an enrichment class; however, when continuing on to middle school after I graduated, there was no mention of this talent and hence moving forward, I lost the opportunity to grow.

◆

I was born in Canada and have faced a lot of difficulties. My parents didn't speak a word of English. Every time I had homework, I would always have trouble not knowing certain things. I couldn't ask my parents for help because they wouldn't comprehend what I was trying to ask them.

I would always be embarrassed by my parents when there would be a meet the teacher night because they wouldn't understand anything. I had to translate what the teacher was saying to my parents. Sometimes I could play it to my advantage. If the teacher would say anything bad about me, I would translate it to my parents as the opposite of what was said.

◆

Four or five years ago, I was speaking with a black man who taught at a school in Etobicoke. He was frustrated because his school's population was something like seventy or eighty percent black, yet the history curriculum was completely based on white history. He asked if he could modify it to include a bit of black history, but was turned down.

This bothered me for two reasons.

One, why is there such inflexibility? No one thinks it would be a good idea to give these students something they can relate to? I guess the Board thinks it makes much more sense to put a lot of resources to set up one Africentric elementary school to serve all of Toronto. Of course, the school is at the corner of Keele Street and Sheppard Avenue West, which isn't exactly convenient for someone living in Etobicoke.

Two, even if a school's population is ninety-five percent white, there should be some black history on the curriculum. Don't we want to expand the minds of all our children? Don't we want to break down barriers? The funny thing is that I don't know how one can teach Canadian history without touching upon a variety of races. It's not like this was an all-white country until recently. For example, blacks have been a part of Canadian history for about as long as white settlers, so how do they get left out of the discussion?

◆

A lot of our students might lack academically because they have different styles of learning. A lot of them are hands on, and that's the way they learn. They don't learn by sitting in a classroom full of thirty students and one teacher who has a curriculum to follow and get through in a certain time.

What about the students who don't pick it up by looking at a board? Why not implement other ways of learning? We need to explore something different. They have space in the schools, as they are gradually sharing space in the schools by giving out permits. That's what we need to encourage. I guess funding is an issue.

◆

It's important to catch people at a time in life when they're going to make choices. Ask them, "What would you like to do? What skills do you have? We can help you capitalize on that."

We need more modelling. Too many boys look at rapping or playing basketball, because that's all they see. There are so many windows that can be opened. Everyone's skills are unique and different. Sometimes you end up losing those skills because you don't nurture them.

The schools are very quick to label kids. Once they see the child can't focus, is not paying attention, is disturbing the class, they label them as behavioural and the kids carry this label through middle school, high school, and the kids also carry this mentally. They go into their adulthood thinking that there's something wrong with them, so why even bother trying?

I know an individual who was specifically labelled as a behavioural problem. This is what she carried through middle school and high school. She never focused, she ended up running away from home and wound up in foster care. They wanted to give her medication like anti-psychotics, and this actually made the situation worse. There was nothing at all wrong with her except she saw the world differently, and she learned in a different way. She wasn't someone who could pick up information by sitting in a classroom.

And if you pick up all that information, how do you implement it? All this stuff goes into your head, and you don't know what to do with it. That's what happened to her. Now she's an adult and she's reversing things, she's able to control her emotions, but it's so challenging to overcome all the labels that have been put on her in the past. I can see that happening to a lot of children now.

If you cram everyone into a classroom, and you have a book and a curriculum and you pack everything into their heads, I guess you've done your job and you hope that they've learned something. Whatever we've been doing clearly isn't working - we still have violence, we still have poverty, and it's a cycle, especially in communities like Jane-Finch.

I've been sitting in the school office and I've seen how the students react to the teachers. It's like the teachers are losing control, and I question why that is. It's not the responsibility of the teachers but at the same time, they are responsible for the education of these kids. The teachers have the kids from nine to three, so between those hours it is their job and their responsibility to see that these kids are fully engaged. Clearly, they're not because they're finding all these things to do that are in a negative light. There's some kind of distraction, a lack of focus.

There are teachers at Brookview Middle School who treat these kids as if they are their own. They know the community, and they know they have to treat the kids as if they're at home. It gets rough sometimes, and you have to deal with these kids the way their parents would deal with them at home.

There was a teacher like that, and none of the kids would step on her toes at all. She knows all their names, and their parents. If a kid acts up, she'll threaten to tell their mother, who they know will deal with them. It's tough love, and that's part of the culture. You have to know the tactics needed to deal with these guys, and use these tactics in a way that they will respect you.

I've seen other teachers who get so frustrated that they lose control and start yelling. You're not going to have these guys listening to you if they know you've lost control. They're really going to take advantage of you when they see this. They're not dumb, they know what's going on.

People don't want to talk about mental health. There's a stigma around it. If the mother has a problem, she's going to pass it down to her kids. Some of the kids have mental health problems. The schools don't deal with it. First, the school should check them when the kids start school - they should have people there to test them. But they've cut too much. Sometimes it's not a big problem, it's not noticeable.

But because it's not taken care of, as they go through school they are called dumb, they get depressed, and then they cause problems. They'll say this kid is bad, but they won't ask why is this kid bad instead of kicking the kid out of school.

I know a woman whose son was kicked out of kindergarten for being disruptive. This was just last year. How can you kick a four year old out of school? It's ridiculous.

In the old days, teachers did it because it was a calling, like being a preacher. Now they do it for the money, they don't care. It's just the money they care about.

There are a few who are not like that. I know one who teaches at Brookview who's really good with her class. Two years ago, when one child didn't come to class, she went and knocked on the door. She told the mother, "Look, this is not like your son to not come to school. I want to know what is going on in his life."

Imagine that. She noticed he was acting up in class, and then he didn't show up. She's helped him with stuff and he really likes her. She knows her kids, so when one comes to school and starts acting up, she picks up right away and knows that something is not right. That's the way the old-time teachers used to be.

◆

Today, the teachers don't care about the children, they only care about the salary.

I would like to see the teachers who teach here come from our community. If the community centres have some jobs or some money, I would love to see the workers come from the community. They know what's going on in our community, not just come every morning for the salary. The people from outside know nothing about us.

◆

It's only in high school that the teachers don't care about the kids.

◆

I think the education system needs to reinvent itself. There are serious concerns with how minorities learn in a school system that does not reflect their culture and their values. Personally, I don't think the way to deal with this is to create a curriculum that reflects a different culture or cultures.

First, there are many different cultures in our school population. Whose culture do we highlight? Second, even if you do reflect some cultures, the reality is that these children will have to go out and make their way in a city comprised of many different cultures. Third, if it can be proven that current scholastic practises are actually harming children of particular cultures, shouldn't the onus be on the school board to change the practises rather than be allowed to use a band aid solution that only helps a small percentage of that particular group?

I propose that the school board develop a curriculum based on common grounds. Regardless of culture, race, background, we are all people. What common goals and dreams do we share? What fundamental skills do our children need in order to thrive?

When I was in high school, I remember that every now and then, a fellow student would step up and ask the teacher if there was any practical purpose to the topic at hand. "Why are we learning this? How is this going to help me in the real world?"

Far too often this would cause the teachers to stumble, as if this was something they themselves had never considered. I'm sure the question was often asked exactly to see that kind of reaction, or just to get a break. Still, there should be a good reason for everything that is taught in school, and teachers should be ready and able to articulate those reasons to the students. As far as I'm concerned, "because it's on the test" is not a good reason.

Is there a practical purpose for what children are being taught? I suggest that if you want to reach children, there's more to it than efforts to reflect their culture.

It's important to show students why this is important to them in terms of their future success. Is this useful to their lives? Does it make them critical thinkers? Does it enable them to express themselves verbally and on the printed page (or screen)?

We need a curriculum that motivates and challenges children of all races, and gives them the skills to make the best of their opportunities. And this has to start at the earliest levels.

We need a "one size fits all" curriculum. By this, I mean one that is designed to appeal to any potential student.

When I went to school, the system reflected a white Anglo middle class setting, which didn't really reflect my own European background. A curriculum for a Toronto school should reflect the entire cultural range. There is this idea that Jane-Finch is made up of one cultural background, but this is not true.

Teachers need to be trained to deal with a wider range of cultures, and not just for "priority" neighbourhoods, either. Every school should reflect the city's wide range of cultures and races, no matter how the local population breaks down. Every student everywhere in this city should have their horizons broadened.

After all, a lot of white Anglo middle class children grow up to be teachers, police officers, lawyers, and other careers that could very likely require them to interact with other races and cultures. Tolerance and understanding should be core principles for everyone. And from a cost standpoint, it's far less costly to do this, rather than try and develop "culture-sensitive" curricula for different schools.

Also, I think a lot more work will go into a curriculum that's aimed at all students. If a curriculum is developed or modified for certain areas, then there will always be a stigma. The children will get the message, "we are teaching you this because we believe you're not really able to grasp material like the children in other schools."

And why assume that all children in Jane-Finch lack the academic skills to succeed? There is a lot of brain potential that we are wasting when we assume the children here just can't cut it.

◆

I notice that as time goes on, the resources that we have become less and less. Even in the places where you thought they'd never touch, like the school board, Ministry of Education, they are taking away resources. For example, the hands on activities for the kids are gone. They don't have wood shop anymore and that's a very good skill, one that could become a trade. This is something the children could benefit from in the future. I can only imagine, if it's like this now, what it might be ten or twenty years from now.

◆

Right now, the kids spend time learning about unnecessary things. The school could have been teaching them a trade so that if they don't get their high school diploma, at least they have a trade they can go into. Or teach something that interests them. Not everyone wants to become a scientist or a doctor. Put some subjects there so that the kids don't have to get a ninety-five to do well. Some of these skills are worth more to them than getting a diploma. They'll get a piece of paper and still have a tough time getting jobs.

I know that you can make a lot of money working as a mechanic. Back in our day, we had automotive class, or shop. If they have these kinds of subjects in school, a lot of the kids who are dropping out now could be taking these classes. They could have been more interested and would have a reason to attend school.

◆

I think the school board needs to recognize what kind of population they're dealing with. I know TDSB is standardized, and some areas are different from others. Here, you're dealing with a place where there are many cultural backgrounds. A lot of people here are hands on people. There are language barriers, for example. There are a lot of challenges when you come to an area like this. A lot of the kids who attend school see these challenges and barriers and they feel like they don't have a fair chance already. They feel like they're forced to keep up with this standardized curriculum and keep their academic levels up. Meanwhile, they have all these hidden talents that they could benefit from if they were allowed to tap into those areas as well.

◆

It shouldn't be either/or. Give the kids options, let them make a choice. It should be very broad - gauge each person's skills. Teachers should able to recommend, but not make judgements or choose for the students. If you notice that a student doesn't learn by looking at a blackboard, you might want to show them a different way of learning, a different way to bring out their skills.

Education is very important. It is the future of our children, and as such it is one of the most vital areas that should be focused on. How do they plan to improve the future for the children in the inner city? How will they improve the programs, the curriculum, the activities, and all those things?

◆

Make the children more rounded, don't limit their options. They've got to know everything. Perhaps a child is mechanically skilled, that doesn't mean the child has to be shunted off to a blue collar level. What if the child wants to run their own mechanic business, or repair shop?

You saw how a few years ago, they tried to close down a number of schools, including one in our area, Shoreham Public School. The intention is to shut down as much as they can in these areas. We had to fight for that school. We have to fight for the resources that go back into the schools. I'm afraid that five or ten years from now, the children in Jane-Finch won't have much to work with because the Board didn't want the school open to begin with. They want to sell the property. That's a scary thought. Some people don't want to deal with it. Others will move away and let the problem stay where it is.

◆

Even when times aren't tough, resources are never equally shared. On some level, there's a cost analysis being done. Someone is looking at areas like Jane-Finch and thinking, "well, it's not like most of those kids have the capacity to go very far." So resources get shifted over to the best and the brightest, just like always. How well has that worked out for society as a whole? How much potential has our society lost by writing off so many as not being bright enough, or being unable to learn?

A few years ago, I read some articles on advances in brain science and how they should be applied to teaching. I don't have the knowledge to lay it all out here, but the key is that brains are basically the same.[2]

When it comes to learning capacity, there's no difference between a male brain and a female brain, no difference between a black brain and a yellow brain. Deep down, we all want to learn.

Think a child is dumb and destined to be an underachiever? Tell me, does that child play video games? Watch how a child bears down and learns how to master a video game, and then try to tell me that child can't learn. It's a matter of finding the right motivation, setting the right environment, and finding relevance in what's being taught.

I said at the start that resources aren't equally shared. What I should have said is that resources aren't equally developed. And by "resources," I mean the minds of our youth. Let's look at the bigger picture. Rather than ask for more money to be put into the same old system that has been underdeveloping so many students, shouldn't be we asking for a system that brings out the learning capacities of every child?

Notes

[1] Westview Centennial Secondary School (755 Oakdale Road) offers Grades Nine to Twelve. The school motto is NOS OMNIA TENTEMUS ~ "Let Us Attempt All Things."

[2] An article that discusses how advances in neuroscience can be applied to education is located here: http://atkinsonfoundation.ca/wp-content/uploads/2013/07/brainstorm-the-secret-to-better-schools.pdf
From the article: "The brain is malleable. And the research is showing that if students think they can learn, then they do. If they think their intelligence is fixed at a low level - whether because of social or economic status, skin colour, gender, family history, which country they live in - then they stick to that level."

My Story - Four (Male)

"The biggest regret of my life is ever giving him a chance."

I don't like my father right now. He was in my life for the first five years and then I didn't see him for over ten years. One day he called out of the blue. He spoke to my brother. When my brother told me who had called, I was in shock. At first, I didn't want to talk to him, telling him I was sick. My mom asked if I could go to his place for dinner. Part of me did want to get to know him a little.

Not having a father is devastating. Without a dad, there's no guidance. That's why kids are in jail, or selling drugs. The father has to have the heavy hand. My mom raised me well. I consider my mom to be both mother and father. I didn't even want him to hear my voice, so when mom was talking to him on the phone I'd use sign language.

I did end up talking to him. He asked do you know who I am? I told him. He said, "good job." What the hell. He didn't say anything about being away, he just acted like nothing happened. I went to see him, it was really awkward. He had a wife and made me say hello to her over a web cam - she's living in another country. That felt strange.

I even slept over at his house. It was a struggle with my feelings, whether I cared for him as a father, or whether I liked him at all. Now the struggle is over - I don't like him. He bought me a phone and a TV, but it's over at his home. He bought the TV so I could use my Playstation. I'd spend the weekend there, but we wouldn't do anything.

I was expecting we would have a good father-son relationship. He overheard me saying I didn't want to be there. He got mad at me, and said I could leave. But if he ever needed me, I'd have to come. When I heard that from him, that was it. I lost respect for him. I made a mistake giving him a chance. The feelings are lost.

Sometimes my mother came with me. I told her I didn't want to be there. Once again he overheard, and said he'd drag me to his place if he needed me. Right now, I wouldn't care if he was alive or dead. If anything happened to my mother, I'd care for days. Feelings are built up over time. My mother was there for me every day. He's lucky I sort of forgave him, but he messed that up. He said, don't make me treat you like my other son. He treats the poor guy like trash.

He was very rude to me. To be honest, he seemed like a person who didn't have empathy. The thing is, he's been married to three different women, divorced all of them, and had children with each of them. We don't know if he has a wife currently, or if he has other kids. He's a mystery, a book you can never read.

The things he'll say to me always anger me. We were on the phone the night before and he told me he bought a house. He bought a house and didn't even have the decency to invite me? I felt disrespected, though I didn't tell him that.

He always criticizes me about my weight, telling me, "too fat!" Why doesn't he take some of the blame? When I was young, he took me out to fast food restaurants and would always buy me combos. He'd never buy me (the smaller) Happy Meals. There are photos of me when I was a young child, and I was skinny - you could see my ribs. Then there are photos of me when I was three and I'm chubby. He spoiled me with that food, so obviously I'd be wanting more.

He's a control freak. He wants to control the way I eat, the way my hair looks, the way my physique is, the way I walk. He can tell me this because he's my dad, but at the same time, at least give me the common courtesy of living my own life. He wasn't in my life for eight years, and now he cares?

When I was younger, I'd always ask my mother, "Where's father? Why isn't he here?"

I don't remember how she answered. I think my mother would tell me she was there for me, but I'd still wonder. There were times he'd come to take me to a movie. But every time, there was a woman with him. I felt cheated because I thought it would be father-son time, but it was always father-son-girl friend time. I told my mother. He said if I ever told my mother anything again, he'd come in the middle of the night and slit my throat. That was very traumatic. I might have been five, maybe four. I never forgot that. That's when I stopped seeing him.

The first night I went there, I could not sleep because I can't sleep in a new bed. It was a weekday, so I was very sleepy. I wanted to go home after school so I could sleep. He didn't care. He's very stubborn - he's always right. If he treated me nice, I'd give him a chance and maybe I could love him. Instead, I'll be respectful to him, but that's it.

Just coming back like that doesn't mean anything. There are some things you can't forgive.

Mom's role is to love you, shelter you, feed you. If the father's not there, then he's there with the wallet, while mother's there with open arms.

I don't remember exactly how I felt when I found out they were divorcing. But I don't think I took it well. I did get used to it being my mother and us. That one phone call changed it instantly.

It's bittersweet. I'm learning a lesson. One day I'll have kids of my own, and I have to be there for them. You never know - your kids might never forgive you. I'm never going to abandon my kids.

He often goes back to his native country but won't tell me when he's coming back. And when he does come back, he doesn't call to let me know. I'll call him and that's how I find out.

We had somewhat of a strong relationship about a year ago, when my mother got back together with him. But now it's slowly fading away. He still has to stay in touch with me every now and then, but it's not like he's a real father to me.

He doesn't call me to see how I'm doing at school - he calls me every other month. And it turns out the main reason my mother got back with him was so I would have a father in my life.

My mother brought him to Canada. If it wasn't for her, he wouldn't be in the position he has now. The money back home doesn't compare to the money he makes in Canada. The currency conversion works really well for him.

I have cousins back home who'll work hard all week for what would be about five dollars for me. They're younger than me, and I don't even have a job. I feel so sorry for them. Whenever I go back to visit, I always give them money, so they can go out and buy chips and stuff like that. I love to make them happy.

Sometimes I believe parents in my religion try to force marriage on their kids. My father was trying to do that to me. No one can block love. If I were to marry outside my religion, my dad would be angry.

I would rather have not answered the phone and left him out of my life. I had a great life with my mother and my brother, but ever since he came in, my father's made it bad with the yelling and the stress. Initially, I thought it would be good to finally bring my father back into my life. I know this sounds harsh, but the biggest regret of my life is ever giving him a chance. I regret bringing him the satisfaction of thinking I love him when I really don't. Seriously, get out of my life.

80

Housing

Various insights into life as lived in public housing.

Background: when we talk about "housing" in this chapter, we mean social housing managed by Toronto Community Housing, or TCH for short. TCH has a large presence in Jane-Finch: there are nine TCH sites in an area starting north at Shoreham Drive, going slightly west of Jane Street, south to Grandravine Drive, and east to Tobermory Drive. The Toronto Community Housing Corporation was incorporated by the City of Toronto in 2000 to manage social housing.

The actual housing has been around much longer. In 1964, the Ontario Housing Corporation (OHC) was created to build affordable housing. A 1958 plan called for 1,500 units to be built in the area later to be known as Jane-Finch. Once the shovels hit the ground, the area experienced a massive population surge in a single decade, going from 1,300 people in 1961 to over 33,000 by 1971.[1] By 1975, just over twenty-two percent of all Jane-Finch dwellings were public housing.[2]

The Jane-Finch project was designed as a reproduction of downtown Toronto's Alexandra Park, and "the internal principles governing both designs were similar - clean, uncluttered, and enclosed space set off from the general community."[3]

How well did the model work? Let's listen to those who live there.

◆

Community housing to me is like an industrial complex. If you look at them from overhead, you're so locked in, so crammed. All this concrete, all these high walls, it's almost like a prison. Police will come into these areas and harass folks, search them, and ask them questions. So you may be living there, but you're never really comfortable or secure. You have to deal with the violence within the walls and you have to deal with the poverty within those walls, and there's nowhere to run within those walls.

◆

I don't like that someone put up signs to identify TCH areas.[4] Now you know which areas to harass. Why would they do that? How are you supposed to feel comfortable living in places like that? It's a big orange and white sign for everyone to know.

We had a friend who lived in an area which we didn't know was TCH. We thought she was better off, living in a townhouse. "Oh you're so lucky, living in houses," but we didn't know at the time that it was TCH. And not knowing built up your self-esteem, thinking your friend could be living there.

Now right at the tip of the driveway there's a big sign telling you it's TCH. Why are those signs there - to show people their tax money at work? They're marking their territory? I guess the police need to know the area now. A lot of people didn't like it.

That kills your pride because people talk down so much on TCH and you're living in subsidized housing. It's transitional housing, so it's a stepping stone to get somewhere. It's not really something bad if it's helping you to get on your feet. Some people do abuse it, and that makes it negative.

◆

How is it transitional housing? People don't leave unless they get kicked out for not paying their rent or something. If you have three children, you might get a three bedroom. If a child leaves, then you get moved to a two bedroom, and so on. You can't come in and ask for a three bedroom otherwise, so they're just accommodating your circumstances. You might be in place for a long time and get comfortable, then you have to move away. That's the transitional part - your kids get set up and leave, and you should be setting yourself up to leave too.

It's hard for some people to leave because if they get a job that pays more, they're scared because now they have to pay more rent while they may not be in a position to do that yet. So maybe they try to keep their income minimal, and that's how you get comfortable with the lifestyle. You're getting subsidized, you're not paying much, you stay at a minimal income, and before you even know it, time has passed on and on, then you find that you haven't been able to save anything.

◆

I went to a meeting a few years ago where residents could discuss housing issues. There was a woman who complained about rent geared to income. She was living in a $800 a month apartment. She started to get overtime at work, and eventually her rent went up to $1200 a month. As she said, "If you came into my place, you'd see it is not a $1200 a month apartment."

How is subsidized housing designed? Is it designed to help a person move up, or is it designed to keep a person down?

◆

You need to have the heart of a lion to break out of that system, to defeat that way of thinking, to get your foot out of the door and pull yourself up out of it. If you're surrounded by it, day in and day out, it becomes the reality. You know in your head, something keeps telling you that you can't do this. You make it what you have to make it while you're there, and I think people should strive to find a way to get out.

People would do so much better if they weren't in housing. They would be able to reach so many more aspects if they weren't worried about not going over income limits so they could protect the amount of rent they're paying. When you're in that space, it's hard to think of reaching out and elevating yourself. If everyone had that drive to overcome the system and not need to depend upon it, they could probably reach places that they didn't think possible.

◆

I went over to the TCH offices because I wanted to get my son off the lease renewal. I was told I had to get a letter of termination from him. This was a new lease, but they said it didn't matter. If he does something wrong, we all have to leave. How is that right? If my daughter wants to leave, she has to give two months notice - that means I have to pay for those two months. Housing is creating a rift between us and our children. We want things to go smoothly, but for them (TCH), it's all or nothing.

My son would have to reapply on his own, so we can't separate. Housing can transfer us all, but not separately. You don't want to tell them anything because you'll get penalized. I want my son to get his own place, where I can give him food and visit him, so he's not on the street. I want him out of my house because now he does what he wants; he needs to be on his own to develop independence.

Because he's home, he doesn't want to do anything, not learn any responsibility, leaving it all to me. If anything happens to me, what happens to him? He's twenty-one and he can't cook or take care of himself. He can't plan, he can't go shopping. My other child is on her own, and she learns how to shop and how to maximize her money.

◆

I was affected by the recent flood (July 8, 2013). My basement flooded, and I had water up to my knees. We lost a lot of stuff, and a lot of things were damaged. After the flooding, the first thing Housing did was take two steps back. They said, it's really tough to be you guys, but you should have had house insurance.

I would have expected Housing to approach the city because the city streets and sewers were not cleaned properly. Therefore, the water couldn't go down. A Good Samaritan went into the street where the water was coming up from, and cleared it amongst all the murky crap, like there was feces and stuff there. He went in there and moved it all so the water could go down. Because the water went down so fast, it had to go somewhere, so it came up in all our houses.

I was without hot water for seven days. When I phoned Housing, I was told to call Enbridge because they didn't have anything to do with it. I replied that in a situation like this, they should have staff calling Enbridge - don't keep throwing your hands up in the air. Then the maintenance man told me, "When Enbridge comes, don't mention the flood. Just tell him that your water heater's not working so he'll try to fix it. We don't want to have to buy it out and pay lots of money."

I told them I would not do that. The reply was if I didn't, then money would have to change hands, it would take a long time, and we don't know when you're going to get hot water. I said, "Okay. I'll go home and call my councillor and I'll talk to you guys on Monday."

The next day, Saturday, they called me first thing in the morning and asked if I was going to be home so they could install a water heater. Now go figure; previously, it was going to take a long time to fix my problem, but when I said I would call my councillor, I got a water heater within twenty-four hours.

I called them about the basement flooding and damaging my stuff. They said, "You're not supposed to live in your basement. You're not supposed to have anything in your basement." Really? So where am I supposed to put the washer and dryer? In my kitchen?

They said, "None of that stuff is our responsibility. You have to take care of that stuff." My stuff isn't damaged because of my neglect. My basement has never leaked, no matter whether it's raining or snowing.

But one neighbour's place leaks due to poor maintenance, and the other neighbour's place leaks on one side. She's made plenty of requests for someone to check her windows because every time it rains, the water goes down into her basement. But nobody comes. When the flooding first started, my basement was fine, while the neighbours were leaking.

After a while, my neighbours asked, "How can that side be flooding, and the other side, but not you?"

I went downstairs and water was up to my knee. So it came in from both sides. If the walls were sealed and maintained properly, then this wouldn't have happened. I'm the victim here.

I had power bars plugged in the basement and they were under water. The power was off when I was down there and when I realized what could happen if the power came back on, I got out of there. I didn't want to be down there touching things so that's why I called TCH.

To this day (two weeks later), they haven't shown up. Everything we did on our own. They haven't shown up to say if it's safe to unplug anything. I filled out a form and no one has come to my place. This is really bad service. The funny thing is that there are ten houses in my row, and the City came to House Seven, to help clean their basement. And that was it.

I lost a lot of stuff. That was basically my son's place in the basement. I was told I was responsible for getting house insurance, but I was told this after the fact. They give us an option to pay for parking, why not have an option to add insurance? Maybe they don't do it because it would put more onus on TCH to maintain their properties. If I went out on my own looking for insurance, would any company offer it to me?

◆

I got a new stove today. Why do I have to get electrocuted four times before getting a new stove?

I got shocked by my stove, and tried to figure out what happened. Then I got shocked again. So I called TCH and told them, "I was shocked by my stove once already. I just got shocked right now and I'm burning, so you guys need to check the stove."

The gentleman came and he said the stove looked fine - maybe my hands were wet when I touched the pot. I said that something couldn't be fine if I can't have wet hands when I touch a pot or I could get shocked. So many people would have been electrocuted by now if that was the case.

So that was his story and I decided, fine, whatever. I got shocked again. The fourth time, I was burning. It felt like I had my hands under hot water. My fingertips, my nose, and my lips were burning. My extremities and my ears had the same feeling like when your foot falls asleep. You just want to rub it and make it stop.

The effects of the fourth shock lasted a few days. So I called TCH and told them I was going to call my councillor. They said they'd send me a new stove in a few days. And they did.

Everything else I've ever received, some touch ups, the new water heater, everything happened because I said I was going home to call my councillor and right away, it got done within a week. I've never called my councillor. That's how you get the service. It's really ridiculous.

◆

TCH has a new law that states if your children do something wrong while living in housing, the family will have to leave their dwelling. If each child over sixteen signs his or her lease, why doesn't just that child leave? Why should the whole family have to vacate the dwelling?

If I want to put that child out it is not possible unless I have a restraining order or the child requests to leave in writing. You see the double standard. It is not fair to tell me to leave my rental because one of the individuals on the lease decided to do something stupid.

Why should my other children and myself be without a home because one of the leaseholders has done something wrong? Why should I pay the price for one of the lease signers? If I kick that person out, I will have to pay their rent until they personally terminate their lease. TCH has the right to make arbitrary decision about who should be terminated from their premises. It sucks. But that is the life of a TCH renter.

◆

I have some concerns with Toronto Housing. A few years ago, they start telling us that we have to pay for anything that gets broken in the place. And it's not like they gave us brand new stuff to begin with. We moved into the house and found fixtures covered with mould, items that were rusting, old-fashioned stuff. And so when the time comes that we need new stuff, they're telling us we'll have to pay for it. The other day, I told them about the toilet and the sink.

Let me talk about the sink. I moved in and found this old-time sink - they don't make those things anymore. So the pipe erupted and fell off. I told them I needed a new faucet. They came over and fixed it and put on a new faucet, but they never tried to scrub all of the stuff because it's a smaller faucet - it's not the same size. So they just put on the new faucet and left all the dirt.

Okay, I'm thinking at least they fixed the sink. A few days later, they put a letter in my mail slot telling me I have to pay them $150 for the faucet. When I looked into it, Canadian Tire was selling that faucet for about sixty-seven dollars. Housing told me that I had to pay for the labour. I'm still fighting it.

Housing tried doing the same thing to me with the toilet. They charged me $350. I went in and complained and they dropped it to $150. I paid it because at that time I did not have much knowledge.

Now there's stuff in my sink that needs to be fixed and I'm scared to call them because they'll tell me I have to pay for it. If these things don't get fixed and I move out of housing, they're going to charge me. So I'm caught up in the middle.

◆

How can you move a person into a place that needs a total make over and expect the tenant to pay for it? It's a rental property. When the renter leaves, it's not like you can take anything back. It should be up to TCH to replace these items.

They're very much aware that these buildings are old. So what was the point of removing the entire TCH Board and starting fresh?[5]

Now they turn around and make the tenants pay for the losses that they (TCH) have had? They made some very bad decisions with the old board, such as going to China to buy fixtures,[6] and transactions that are not accounted for, and all these different things so I guess they've got to get the money back from somewhere.

◆

I've been a tenant rep for four or five years now, and I've never seen a single dollar for repairs in my neighbourhood. TCH sends me a letter asking if the fridge is still working in our community kitchen and we don't even have a community kitchen. If we do, I don't know anything about it - maybe the staff uses it. Why are they calling me about this when they won't talk to me about the annual budget?

I went in and I fought to get new doors for the place, and I didn't even get a thank you. All I did was get a new front door. So where is all this money that we're supposed to get for our community? I don't see the barbecues and all of that.

◆

I attended the TCH meeting where it's set up so that the tenants have to compete to get funding for their area. These areas are lacking in many ways. They need a lot of repairs as things are falling apart. TCH has this pool of money that they set aside every year, and all the TCH properties are supposed to come together and try to compete for it.

It's not a good way of handling things because you're condoning what's going on in the streets because it's a similar mindset. Maybe they haven't really thought about it that way, but making tenants compete against one another is something that causes division. Yet we're in the same community and supposed to be united.

It might be subsidized rent, but they're still paying it, so they shouldn't have to be fighting each other to get funding. Some of these people are unsuccessful, so they go back empty-handed and repairs don't get made. And this is where people have to live.

Naturally, these environments aren't healthy so these kids will have side effects. Their living circumstances are poor, the effect is mental, and they're going to conduct themselves in the same manner.

I've gone to those meetings and there's people present who I like to refer to as celebrities - whatever they ask for, they get. So you're fighting for no reason at all because TCH already knows who they're giving the money to. Still I fought to get the doors.

A lot of people were upset that I just came to the meeting. I was surprised by all the animosity in the room. Those meetings make me uncomfortable because of how they're set up.

Tenants should be entitled to get these renovations as needed. Yes, it's government property but if a private landlord owned the building, it's their duty to improve their building and not let it get run down. That's what happens when tenants pay their rent - you take a portion of that for repairs. I'm sure these buildings were paid off a long time ago. So there should be money to pay for repairs, but it's not happening.

A lot of the tenant reps just give up because of all this battling. "We need new doors, no *our* building needs new floors" - it's this back and forth. You have to wait four rounds (years), because if you got new floors last year, you're definitely not getting anything fixed this year.

And yet I see that the celebrities get whatever they want. So some communities are well off, at least more so than the communities that are not so popular at these meetings.

◆

In this community, most of the TCH buildings look very old. They're in desperate need of repairs. They need a revitalization. It was said that they were going to go to Shoreham (Edgeley Village Shoreham) and do some type of revitalization, but I guess the community is the last to find out about those things.

I think it would be more cost-effective to tear this housing down and rebuild because they keep spending all this money on repairs while the places keep breaking down. It's like putting on band-aids.

I ended up moving out of Shoreham because I couldn't take it any more. We had a contractor come in because there was a leak. He knocked down the walls and the pipes had holes. He took one look at those pipes and he became so frightened.

He said those pipes were ridiculously old and they don't even use that kind of material any more to make pipes. So to be living in a place where the pipes aren't even being made any more, you can only imagine what the insides of the walls are like.

And that makes me think about health concerns because a lot of people living in these places are getting ill. The people complain of mould and all these different problems. It's clear why this is happening because they're living in places where you might not be able to see the mould, but it's there.

Talking about mould, there was a leak in my washroom and you could see the mould on the walls. I started to watch health films, so I had knowledge of mould.

When the contractor came, I pointed out the mould and told him to fix it or I'd call the Board of Health. So he said he'd fix it. He must have talked to TCH because the next day, when I came home, you know how they fixed it? They tried to paint over it.

It looked nice on the first day, but on the second day, the mould reappeared. That's how you guys got rid of it? They're supposed to have enough knowledge to know that it's going to come back. They don't want the hassle. It's always band-aids and quick fixes.

Some people don't know what mould does. You need a more educated community on those topics.

I'm sure that if more people in the community would complain about the mould, they would have no choice but to fix it. They don't want word to get around that these places have mould and people could get sick.

Mould could be a big problem. They still have to answer to Health and Safety, or someone could call the Fire Department and tell them to come check this. Now you have another problem on your hands because the building has been called a health hazard.

If people are willing to take it to that extent, then they would have to make those changes. But it's a task where you feel defeated - it's their property so you don't even consider that you're paying rent. Yes, it's subsidized but we're still giving them a portion of the rent, so we do have a right to speak on the behalf of our well-being.

We're afraid that if we do speak out, they'll evict us. There are consequences if you use your voice. Or maybe they try to pull you away as an individual and buy you off to keep you quiet - that's what they usually do. They'll give you this or give you that, keep you quiet, try to make things look nice.

And when you look at the bigger picture and look at what you're dealing with, it's not just my building. There are so many other places that have the same issues. Am I willing to deal with all this? After all, this is the government. Can I manage to take on the government? Everyone's fearful of doing that.

◆

They say that people who live in the Jane-Finch area suffer from higher rates of ill health. They're in and out of doctor's offices and hospitals because they're sick. There's many reasons for this, and poor housing would be one of them.

◆

Community housing is not as communal as one might think. In community housing, there's a lot of back-biting going on.

When I first moved into community housing, I didn't really engage with others very much. That was because I had heard so much about living in TCH - how people behaved, the violence, all those images that were pressed into my mind by what people said.

So for the first few years, I would mainly stay inside, go out of the area to the bus stop and go back. Then a couple of years later, I started engaging with one or two neighbours and getting out there, exploring what was going on in the community.

I don't know if that was such a great idea. Of course you got to know people, but at the same time, now you find yourself in a lot of community arguments and community mix ups.

This person feels they have more seniority in the area than that person has. There's a lot of bickering. If there's an event, there's all this animosity - people can't seem to get along because this person feels like they should be in charge, and that person should be in charge. It just gets so technical with the people there. It was a turn-off after a while.

◆

When you get engaged in the community and get to know people, you get to know a main person who would tell you about everyone else in the community. And then you would get the image in your head not to talk to this particular person, to stay away from that person. So you would not want to get involved with these people because you already have a history for them.

I don't know if every TCH development is like this, but you have one person who might be the "warden." They have access to every unit. They're a key holder, they know everybody.

Once you get to know that warden, they come to your home and you share things with them. That person may not be the most trustworthy. That person will take everything they learn and bring it to others. After a while, your privacy is gone. It up and vanished after you got engaged with the community.

If there's an event happening in the community, and it happens that the warden is the one who's controlling it, no one else really wants to get involved because if you step on the warden's toes, you probably won't get any more resources. If they allocate resources through her and she's the person to give it around, she might skip your door.

There are all these little minor things you have to deal with in TCH housing. I know people who don't want to participate because this warden is in control of everything that happens.

Just to be clear, the "warden" is not the tenant rep. If it was, it would probably make some sort of sense. Not that it would be okay, but at least we have some say in that because we vote for them.

Instead, they tend to have the rep under their control. They do everything for the tenant rep, and so they get access to everything. If something is being given out like free doors, and you're not good to this warden, you're not getting a door. I say "free," but it's something you're entitled to get. Only something happens and suddenly you're not getting a door. And you wonder why.

I don't know how that's going to change. These wardens are people who have lived there for years. They grew up there from when they were kids. And that affects the community greatly, because when other people want to come in with resources, these people are very territorial.

They're not open to outside resources coming in and trying to help out. Instead they feel like these outsiders are coming to take over. So they make it bad for the rest of the community. And I'm speaking from experience. Someone from outside wanted to bring in a program, but because there are these wardens who sit on the council for the community, they don't make it easy for those coming from outside. They want to be in control of it, and if they can't be in control, then the community just doesn't get anything.

Being on the outside, you definitely wouldn't know or see it, because there were a lot of things that I didn't know about TCH until I actually moved into it. So I was happy to go through the experience, so I know what I might not want to have to deal with again on that level.

◆

I didn't know generations were raised in TCH - that's the norm! Grandmothers raised their kids and then those kids raised their kids. It's like a cycle. I thought it was temporary housing, somewhere to stay until you get on your feet, but it's like they've given up hope.

They've raised their kids until they're grown and those kids are still living there, only now with their kids. When is the hope coming for a better life? It's like that's their world. How they think, how they feel, it becomes their existence. Anything government related, if they can get any support, this is what they rely upon. They work and they try to keep their work to a minimum so they don't go above that rate where you have to end up being independent and doing things on your own.

If you can get subsidized housing, that's fine, which they say is transitional housing, only I don't know how true that is if you've been there for years. You have social assistance and that becomes an existence for them, and those are the ones who become "wardens" in the area because they don't think they're going anywhere.

They become territorial and they don't seem like they want to leave. They've been there so long they don't know what's out there in the real world. They're one-minded. When people try to bring in resources, they think they're trying to take over. They're intimidated by anything new, anything that takes away their control.

They don't want to hear anything about mixed income, about breaking this community down and making it mixed income. I've had some debates in the backyard and in the courtyard over mixed income. They are not willing to accept it at all. They fear they'll lose their space, they fear that the rent will go up.

I try to explain to them that mixed income is good because people won't know who is subsidized and who isn't. If you're living next door to somebody who isn't subsidized, then it's inspiration and motivation for you to go out there and do something and climb up and become someone who is not subsidized.

Otherwise, when you're around this constantly, day in and day out, you're not wise enough to come above it, you get used to it. It becomes your lifestyle. People adapt to the environment and they forget that there is so much going on outside that bubble. At times I felt very stagnant living in TCH, being in that environment.

If I was stuck in the situation where I lived near a warden, that would give me so much motivation to get out. The warden had access to everything, so if you knew her and were on good terms with her, you were good. But if you weren't, it wasn't good.

The warden was like a rooster. As soon as it was light, she was up and talking away. There was no privacy. Once you went and engaged in everything, there'd be rocks outside your window. It was very stifling.

◆

When you hear "community housing," you think it means everybody contributes towards the community. I thought it would be like co-op housing, where everyone mows the lawns, everyone takes part to make the community a better place.

When they say "community housing" in TCH, that's more like you've lost your sense of privacy because everybody's watching and everybody's talking. If you get a new door, everyone will want to know why you got a new door.

They'll want to find out everything they need to know. Everyone's trying to get what they can get. That's the reality at TCH.

It's not the easiest place to live. Some people don't even come out of their house because they don't want to deal with the tenement yard. You won't even see them in their backyards. "Tenement yard" is a Jamaican term - you go outside into the yard and it's like you're inside everyone's house. Going to sit in your backyard is like sitting in the courtyard of some institutional facility. There's too much shared space.

We're so close you can hear the people through the walls, "Shut up, your music's playing too loud!" The walls are paper thin.

If you're at all different, you definitely become the minority within your community. If you don't walk like everybody walks, don't talk like everybody talks, sometimes it's best to just keep it to yourself. Better to go chill at a friend's house until it passes.

If you want to elevate yourself, you might want to keep that to yourself, unless there's other like-minded people. Otherwise, there'll be people who'll say, "Come sit in the backyard for twenty minutes," and you'll be there all day.

You can't leave your house without hearing, "Where you going? What time you coming back? Who you going with? What are you going to buy?"

You go buy something, and come back, then it's, "What did you buy?" Like I said, it's very stifling. It's community housing in every aspect. It's very tight.

Notes

[1] John Sakamoto, "How Jane-Finch was born," *Toronto Star*, November 30, 1986.

[2] Julie-Anne Boudreau, Roger Keil, Douglas Young. 2009. *Changing Toronto: Governing Urban Neoliberalism*. Toronto: University of Toronto Press.

[3] "Metro's Suburbs In Transition: Background Report April 1979," Social Planning Council for Metropolitan Toronto.

[4] These signs may not be posted any more. The editor drives past one TCH location regularly and the sign hasn't been there for a while. This doesn't change the tone of the sentiments expressed.

[5] In March 2011, all members of the TCH Board were either persuaded to resign or were moved out after a vote by Toronto City Council. The TCH CEO was fired shortly afterwards. This was the result of an auditor's report.

[6] From the city auditor general's report on the inner workings of TCH: "Thirty-seven separate purchase orders totalling nearly $3 million were issued over a span of eighteen months for procuring various kitchen, bathroom and lighting fixtures from the China-based supplier. In one month, six purchase orders with a value of over $700,000 were issued and two months later a further $700,000 in purchase orders were issued."

"A flooring replacement tender for nearly $2 million was awarded in the form of twenty separately issued purchase orders."

"Expenditures in 2009 for entertainment at one restaurant downtown which totalled almost $5,000. These expenditures were approved by the individual who incurred the expense."

"A cheque of $8,500 for expenses for an event was issued to an employee in July of 2009. To date, no expense report has been submitted to account for the spending of the advance. Consequently, there is no record on what this $8,500 was spent on." ("Fiorito: Heads should be rolling at TCHC," *Toronto Star*, 01 March 2011)

My Story - Five (Female)

"I hate not having control over my own life."

Jane-Finch is a beautiful community. I enjoy living here. I don't have to go far to get things, because there are so many stores within walking distance.[1] There's also clinics and a hospital.

On the other hand there are things that bother me, and one of them is racism. When I moved to this community, I got involved with local organizations. When I did outreach, I went to a house and a white woman answered. She looked scared and she was rude when I asked her questions. I told her that I was here doing outreach and she just closed her door in my face. Since I've been in the Jane-Finch area, I've seen so many of the white people move out.

The things that give me pause are the police, Children's Aid, and Toronto Community Housing (TCH). The police and Children's Aid give me pause because of the power they have over our lives and TCH gives me pause because of the power they have as to whether we have somewhere subsidized to live or not.

I hate not having control over my own life and that of my children. At any given time, anything can happen. I can lose my rental, go to jail, or have my children go into the system. It is depressing.

We have children that we can barely control because the government gives them more rights than they give to parents. So these children get out of control because they think they have the power to make stupid decisions that later affects the whole family, especially the parents if the children are underage.

The law states that the children have rights. When the children mess up, the police have the right to arrest them and depending on what the children did, such as stealing, the parent(s) have the right to pay for their children's thievery.

Being a person of colour makes it one hundred percent harder to control our children in a society that deems them bad because of the colour of their skin. Their situation is compounded more because of where they live.

The sad part about my life is that my children let me fear. I fear that something will happen to them outside of my control. It hurts to feel powerless to control your own existence. When my children were born, I feared that if anything should happen to them I would not be able to help them. As soon as I mastered that fear, another one crept in.

My children are high needs kids. One has Autism (Pervasive Developmental Disorder Not Otherwise Specified) and the other has ADHD (Attention Deficit Hyperactivity Disorder) and ODD (Oppositional Defiance Disorder) plus severe anger.

It has been difficult raising them by myself. Living in this community with so many social agencies made it a little easier to find the resources to help them.

Being educated in the social work field made it a little easier for me to know where to look for the information and find resources. Nonetheless it was hard and is still hard raising them. The umbilical cord is still attached. When it will be severed I do not know.

I can't afford to fall apart. When can I sit back and relax?

My mother left us in Jamaica when I was eight. She went to work in Canada in the 1970s as a domestic. She was working for a white family, watching their kids. They called her "monkey" and all kinds of names. My mother was a very proud person, and she told them off. Her employers said they were going to call Immigration.

She said, "Go ahead and call Immigration. Don't think I'm afraid to go back to Jamaica. That's where my kids are and I have food and a house to go back to."

That's what a lot of these employers would do with the domestics. They knew these women were poor, and they came here to work and support their families. These women would take any crap, and they would tell themselves, "I need to work, I need to think about my family back home," and all that.

My mother was not afraid. She called her employer and said, "I won't let anyone call me a monkey. Come and get your kids."

The employer said, "Don't dare leave my kids. If you leave them alone, I'm going to call the police."

My mother replied, "I would not leave your kids. I'm waiting for you to come home."

So my mother left, and she did not even get paid. She went to Immigration to leave Canada. When you're angry, you can make choices you'll regret later. The officials told her to think about it. Because Canada needed domestic workers at that time, she got her landed status. Trudeau came to the rescue and gave a lot of domestics and others their landed status.[2]

These women had it double tough because the children they left back home resented them. I remember that I never liked my mother. I was thinking, "You leave us, and you call yourself a mother to your kids?"

When I studied about the domestic workers, I found a lot of the children of domestic workers resented and hated their parents for leaving them at the mercy of relatives. Their mother wasn't there to take care of their emotional and physical needs. People don't see that. They only see these women as workers to be exploited.

My mother would come back home every now and then to visit. Everything changed, because it was a one hundred percent readjustment for all of us every time she would return. When my mother was gone, I was the one who had to take responsibility for the family. Being the oldest was hard. I had to wash the clothes, cook, and take my brothers and sister to the doctor. I was very tall for my age so I would have to pay adult bus fare instead of child's fare when I was twelve.

When my father went to work, he would lock us inside the house. In Canada, Children's Aid would be called and we would be taken into care. As a single father with limited funds, what was he supposed to do?

I was twelve going on thirteen and in Grade Seven. I knew where the key was but not allowed to unlock the door when he was not there. Some would judge him as a bad father but only the people who knew what was waiting for us girls would understand why he locked us in.

When I was younger, I heard my friend's sister getting raped and to this day I can still hear her screams.

That's one reason why I don't like men.

I don't have any friends my age because I'm not comfortable with people my age. This started back when I was young. I spent most of my time playing with children younger than me - the Peter Pan Syndrome. Think about this: I was eight when my mother left Jamaica and I became responsible for taking care of three siblings younger than me, with the youngest being three years old. I became an adult while still a child craving for the days when I could go outside and play like my friends.

Even to this day I spend more time with younger age groups than I do people my age. I feel uncomfortable in their company. They seem so old, not only in looks but in behavior. I think and function as an adult, it's just that this other side of me is childish. My daughter always tells me to act like an adult and I always ask her, what does that looks like?

Her friends always come to talk to me about issues they are having and I try to help them. My daughter gets upset because her friends' parents do not do that. They always get mad at her because they say that they wish I was their mother because they can relate to me and I to them.

I learned while I was here that Canada is a country that is not easy to survive in. If you have a job where you are now, don't come to Canada. Your education won't mean much here, the same for your qualifications. A good plan is to come to Canada, make money, and go home. The first time I went back to Jamaica to visit, I couldn't wait to go back home, and "home" for me was Canada. But after you are made to feel unwanted here, Jamaica becomes home and Canada becomes just some place to stay for a while.

You have to struggle for acceptance. Even in Jamaica, if you're white with straight hair, you're okay. If you're brown with straight hair, you're okay; if you are dark skinned with straight hair, you are accepted, at least more than those with wooly hair.[3] It's Colonialism at work. Within our own group, we're very classist towards each other. People spend more time with individuals in their own class than the other.

Whenever I go back to Jamaica, I need someone to translate for me. I am told that I'm not Jamaican because I don't sound like one, and I don't act like one. As children, we were beaten by our aunt if we didn't speak proper English. We couldn't speak Patois around her. She was a well-educated woman. Patois was seen as a lower class language. When I came to Canada and saw the different nationalities speaking other languages I felt excluded because I only knew English.

Years later when I found out that Patois was a language of its own, I was so proud. I learned it just so that I could speak something other than English. Now I felt proud that we have something that no one else has. I would go to college and tell everyone that Patois is a language and not "broken English" as they have a tendency to call it.

I came to Canada in 1982 with my brothers and sister, after years of my mom trying to bring us over and my dad refusing. He did not want his sons to be here because they might be drafted into the army.[4]

It was hard just being the eldest. I wanted my mother to be home with her children. My mother kept trying to get us to join her in Canada by sending my grandmother to convince my dad but nothing happened for a while.

One day while searching for the keys to let us out of the apartment, I found the application forms. I told my dad that I wanted to go to my mother and he told me why he did not want to send us. I thought that was not a good reason for not sending the rest of us plus it would take years for my brothers to be of age to go into the army.

I took the application form to my aunt and she told my father to send us to our mother. She told him that I was getting older and needed to go or else I might get pregnant with no prospect of a good education. Being very smart I told him that he did not have enough money to send me to college. He gave in, partly also because around that time there were a lot of killings going on in Jamaica because of the elections.5

My aunt, being well educated, did all the work. We got all our passport pictures taken and got our passports and went to the Canadian embassy. In comparison to the American embassy, which was across the street from the Canadian embassy, there were very few people at the Canadian embassy. It was clean and beautiful.

We got our documents to travel and all five of us left the island on May 1, 1982. We got our landed status at the airport or it became official there. We were happy to leave and come to this country. I have no regrets coming here. I love Canada but I am weary of the people around. I love its natural beauty. Whenever I go back to Jamaica, I appreciate Canada more; it's not because I think Canada is better than Jamaica, it's just because it is different.

My father came to Canada two years later. He hated being in Canada. In Jamaica all you heard about was America and how it was the best place to be in those days. Canada was the ice country.

My father came to Canada. He wanted to go to America so badly because most of his brothers and sisters were there. He would argue with my mom about coming to Canada rather than America.

When my uncle died and we had to go to America, my father was apprehensive because he does not like to travel. He saw America, at least the part we went to, which was Connecticut. We saw zinc fences, broken down buildings, vacant lots, and, worst of all, the blatant segregation. We asked why we did not see this or that kind of people and we were told that each group of people lived in their own section of the state.

We took buses and we saw no white people. I was shocked. I was used to seeing all types of people in Toronto: black, Chinese, Indian, Jewish, and others. Think of the impact that had on us. After that visit, my dad did not argue with my mother any more about her not migrating to America and taking him there. He has never been back there either. Thank God.

The year I came to Canada I had turned eighteen years old. I went to high school. They gave me about ten to fifteen credits towards my high school diploma. My first year I took some Grade Nine and Ten subjects; I went up to Grade Thirteen. I worked that summer and then I went to college taking Computer Programing and Analysis. I did not finish. I kept failing some of my core courses plus I was getting sick because I am asthmatic.

Also, I did not know that I was a visual learner. It was very hard to learn certain things. Most times when individuals are speaking to me, my mind goes blank. I cannot see or understand what they are talking about.

While I was going to university, I discovered the type of learner I am and then I learned how to understand what individuals are saying.

In order for me to understand anything anyone is saying, I need to have to have a visual image of what they are saying or else it is blank in my head. While in school I had to read one sentence over and over again so I could get a visual image in my head.

When I read stories, I can see what is happening in these stories. I can see anything they describe in my head. I can also physically feel the pain of each individual in my head. The pictures created are so real that I can read these stories once and can describe everything in the book. The images are so sharp that sometimes I have to skip some descriptive words because of the physical impact it has on me.

My grandmother died over twenty-two years ago. Just mention her name and I can remember the day I buried her. I can tell you how she looked, how she smelled, all the people who were there, the church services and the burial service, by just closing my eyes.

I do not just see these images but it is as if it is just happening all over again each time I think about a situation or a person. I failed at school not because I did not know the material but because the information did not create a visual image in my head.

Another thing I learned about myself is that I do not have a lot of friends because my head gets crowded. My head is like a collage and the more people in it, the more I get stressed. I feel better when I am by myself and I never feel lonely.

I never understood all that until I was in university. If I had known that, I would not have left college and worked. I got pregnant and had my first child. He was born with a cone head due to the forceps delivery. When he turned three and had to go to school, I found out that he had ADHD and Autism. A couple of years later I got married and had a daughter who I later found out had ADD (Attention Deficit Disorder), ODD (Oppositional Defiance Disorder), and Aggression.

Five years after my last child was born I went back to school. I took upgrading at Seneca College south of Jane Street and Wilson Avenue. In September of that year, I went to Seneca at the Sheppard Campus taking the Social Service Worker Diploma Program.

Two years later I had a choice between Ryerson and York University. I chose York because it was easier to commute. My children were in daycare and I had to be there by 6:00 p.m. at the latest. I have degrees in Sociology, Psychology, and Social Work with Honours.

Mental illness plays a pivotal role in my family. It is the most debilitating thing that I have ever experienced. I have seen it all my life and I hate it. My uncle had mental illness. He would drink kerosene oil and dig at his skin to remove the bugs he said were crawling inside his skin. I hurt for him. I feel for all individuals who have mental illness.

I do not think many individuals think about the impact mental illness has on the immediate families of those individuals. I feel lost and alone when my daughter suffers from mental illness. She went from being a vibrant individual to a zombie type person. I like her better this way because she gives me less trouble but it hurts.

Trying to get help for her was the hardest thing I have experienced.

I went to the Justice of the Peace and was refused because my daughter was not hurting herself or was a threat to others - except to me, of course. I went to the doctor but because she had not seen my daughter in over a year, it was another refusal because the doctor feared my daughter might sue her.

I took her to the hospital and after hours of waiting, the doctor told her about outpatient help. I objected to that because I knew she would not go and see a psychiatrist on an outpatient basis.

As it turns out, she did not see one and she just got worse. She destroyed the house and hurt me. She called the police and got to go to the hospital. I told them she hurt me because I knew she needed help and they saw that too. The police are also frustrated with the mental health system because most of the time it requires them to arrest an individual when all the person needed was help, not jail time.

I could have had my daughter arrested on many occasions for destruction of property and assault but I did not because I knew she needed help. I knew if I had gotten her arrested there would be no mental health help for her, only a criminal record. What would that solve? It never helped me in the past; the present would be no different.

I had such dreams for both of them. My daughter wants to be a pediatrician and my son wants to be an artist. All their dreams have been derailed for now. My son is trying to get a job so that he can pay off his student loan and also go back to college. He is kind of confused right now as to what he wants to do. It is hard for him just to exist.

It has been hard work for me to keep on telling him how to survive. He is always saying he wants to kill himself if he fails at anything. I have to encourage him, teach him that most of life is about learning and adapting to each circumstance. The good thing is that he owns the suggestions I give to him so it has been successful. But it is hard to keep on doing it.

I do not know what will happen when he does not come to me first when he gets depressed about a failure. I am getting older and sicker each day. If I'm not around, will someone be there for him when he needs that reassurance?

I think that I am cursed. Now my daughter is mentally ill. She is so doped up on drugs that she looks like a zombie. Tears come to my eyes whenever I see her. She is a lost child trying to find her way back to our reality. She has always been a lost child. I quit one of the jobs I had because she would get into so much trouble that it was easier to stay home with her. I had to spend time in the justice system because of her. I work part-time so that I can be home with her.

As time goes by my family increases. I went from two children to five children. I am the legal guardian of my daughter's three children. Taking care of the two eldest ones is like taking care of the two youngest ones, who are two and one years old.

Now the two eldest ones have moved out and I have to take care of them as if they lived at home. I cook and wash their clothes every week. My son is learning to cook and shop for himself with a little support.

My mother helps me a lot when she is in Canada. I could not do without her. She cooks, cleans and takes care of the young ones for me so that I can take a rest. I need that rest.

We as a society should take care of each other instead of beating each other down. We see individuals on social assistance as parasitic and we think they are lazy and do not want to work. I personally find it easier to work than to get assistance from the government.

You do not know the indignities individuals suffer asking for help. Sometimes circumstances dictate the road you travel. Before you judge someone, take a good look at their life and ask why they take the path they take. Try to understand even if you would have made a different decision and taken a different path. I am writing a book about my experiences. I started years ago but have not finished.

Notes

1 Shopping is plentiful in the Jane-Finch area. The actual intersection has malls located diagonally across from each other - the Jane-Finch Mall in the southeast corner, and the Yorkgate Mall in the northwest. There is a large shopping plaza in the southwest corner as well. The Yorkwoods Plaza is no more than a kilometre south of Finch Avenue West on the east side of Jane Street. Residents in the northern section of Jane-Finch have a plaza located on the northwest corner of Jane and Shoreham Drive, just a kilometre and a half north of Finch.

2 The relationship between Canada and domestic workers from the Caribbean is a long one. The Caribbean Domestic Scheme (1910-1911) brought 100 Guadeloupean women to Quebec to work as domestics. The West Indian Domestic Scheme was established in 1955, setting a quota of 280 women a year. Each country had an allotment, with Jamaica getting 104 spots,

and the rest divided among other Caribbean nations. The women had to meet a number of requirements. Once accepted and in Canada, they were given landed immigrant status. Under Prime Minister Pierre Trudeau, immigration policies were modified, particularly between 1973 to 1978. The results would be notable: "In 1966, 87 percent of Canada's immigrants had been of European origin, while only four years later 50 percent came from quite different regions of the world: the West Indies, Guyana, Haiti, Hong Kong, India, the Philippines, and Indochina. Throughout the 1970s and 1980s, newcomers would more often than not have emigrated from Africa, Asia, the Caribbean, or Latin America." (http://preview.tinyurl.com/mk4nlrh)

Here are the recollections of another JFOTM member regarding her mother's life as a domestic worker in Canada: "It was very hard when you came to Canada in the 1960s. White people had to sponsor you. My mother was sponsored, and came over just so she could work for the one woman. Her social insurance number started with nine. Those numbers were used so everyone would know you were sponsored, and they could turn you in if you left your sponsor and tried to get a job somewhere else."

"I knew a woman who ran off from her sponsor. She went to a restaurant to look for a job, they saw that number nine on her card and they called immigration. After they caught her, they took away her passport and gave her a few months to leave."

"When my mother's employers' kids grew up, she wasn't a landed immigrant. She got her landed immigrant status and then her employers let her go have her life. She brought all the family over."

Concerning the social insurance numbers, "SINs that begin with a '9' are issued to temporary workers who are neither Canadian citizens nor permanent residents." (This is from the Government of Canada web site, located at: http://www.servicecanada.gc.ca/eng/about/reports/sin/employers.shtml)

3 This is probably self-explanatory. "Wooly hair" describes hair that is very curly, so much that it almost feels like a sheep's wool.

4 Canada has never had a draft in peacetime.

5 The Jamaican general election held on October 30, 1980, saw the Jamaica Labour Party (JLP) defeat Prime Minister Michael Manley and the People's National Party (PNP) fifty-one seats to nine. Manley had been in power since 1972. The nine months leading to election day was marked by political violence, with over 800 people killed.

Police

"We would love to work with you guys, but we can't trust you."

Living in Jane and Finch, the police visit more often; therefore, if the youths are getting into mischief there is more chance they will be seen. The youths get stopped more often and will get arrested for minor things that they could be warned about or do some community service if they lived somewhere else.

It is hard to send my son even to empty the garbage because of the fear of the police bothering him. If I send him to empty the garbage, especially at night, I will watch him while he empties the garbage.

I think I fear the police more than I fear God. God is fair; the police, on the other hand, will do to you what they please and the system tends to favour the police more than us even when they are lying.

It is not just going to court that is the problem but the whole process: being arrested, having to find a guarantor, and going to court all the time. The worst part is the fact that you will be in the system so that each time you want to travel to the United States you have to explain that charge. The police have the power to make your life miserable.

I used to work night shift, from four to midnight, as a single mother taking care of my two children. To get home, I'd have to catch three buses just to get in the door every morning around two thirty a.m.

There were some community meetings about an increase of muggings and robberies, so they decided to place more police officers in the community. The officers were on bikes, in cars, and during the day, on horseback. It was working because it was deterring the youth that were stealing, etc., from the community. I was happy to hear that!

One morning, I got off my last bus (of the three) and started walking into my community, into my home. This was about a seven to ten minute walk. This particular morning I saw three police cars turn onto the street that I was walking on. My usual routine was to call someone so if anything were to happen to me, help would be sent ASAP. But not this morning! I saw the three cars and told myself I need not bother anyone tonight because the police are here driving slowly to serve and protect! I put my cell in my pocket and began walking with no fear.

Just then one of the police wound down the window and flashed a bright light in my eyes. So did the next car, and then the last. Then one of the police said, "Hey you black bitch, can I take you for a ride?"

I froze. The first thing that came to mind was to call someone and get help. So I reached into my pocket and then I was told not to make a move or I will know what a bullet in the back feels like!

Oh my gosh! It looked like a gun was being pointed straight at me! My heart and mind were racing! I believed I was going to be kidnapped, raped, or killed. My children flashed before my eyes, tears ran down my face which blurred my vision. I told myself to just keep walking!

They all drove slowly beside me jeering n****r, black bitch, wondering what my chocolate body parts would taste like! As if it couldn't get worse, they started riding the curb with their cars telling me that if I ran I would regret it.

I kept trying to look for a car number or license plate. They knew what I was trying to do, and they made sure I was like a deer caught in the headlights - I couldn't see anything! A couple of times, the officers ran the curb trying to scare me with the car - hell yeah, I was terrified!

My mind was going a mile a minute, did they know me, know my kids? Do I pass by my home so they won't know where I live? What do I do? The only thing that came to mind was I just had to see my children! Once I got into my yard my fear became if they were going to let me off so easily. I was trying so desperately to find my house key (OH GOD HELP ME). The last thing that they said was, "Don't worry, we know where to find you!"

I went inside my home slowly, like NO SUDDEN MOVES. I slowly locked the door behind me! I ran to each one of my children's rooms and came downstairs and cried like a newborn baby for hours! Why me? What else could I have done? Will they ever return? What do I teach my children about the police? That they are there to serve and protect?

Let me tell you, as expensive as it was, I took a taxi home every night after that, and I also begged my boss to change my shift. I suffered financially and emotionally for being a victim of such an awful event.

I still wonder when those men get together, what conversation might they have about what happened that night? I know when I think about that night, it's nothing but tears!

I work hard, pay my taxes, the government hires these people to serve their community and protect me, a woman walking home at such late unsafe hours! When I told this to a friend, her response was, "Girl, you should have called the police!"

Really? To do what, serve and protect me?!

◆

TAVIS[1] was supposed to be there to build relationships between the police and the community, but it sure doesn't seem that way. When they first got access to go into the community, it became harassment sessions.

And then after meetings with the community, things simmered down a little bit. They started coming in respectfully and greeting people in a well-mannered way.

I guess as time goes on, there are no more meetings with the community the way it used to be. They fall back into the same cold-hearted habits. No one's really saying much, and no one's really watching them.

◆

There were some police walking around, say a month ago (summer of 2013). I guess they were supposed to be doing community engagement. There's this disabled boy that lives not far from me. There's something wrong with his foot and he's been sick these days. He was smoking weed in front of his door, and the police saw him. Rather than engage with him, they started using their force, saying, "You HAVE to talk to us, you HAVE to let us search you, and you HAVE to do this."

So people called me to come see what was going on. I asked, "Is there a problem here, officer?"

And they responded, "Stay back, stay back, we'll tell you what's going on after we're done!"

"Excuse me? I'm the tenant rep around here. This is my community and I need to know if you guys are trespassing. What's the problem?"

Afterwards, I found out that he's getting arrested for resisting arrest. And they didn't say it then, but he was also being arrested for smoking a spliff (marijuana). I told them I was taking this to the next TAVIS meeting because people couldn't trust the police because they abuse their authority, and they use aggressiveness to try and control the people.

After a while, they were dragging him because he didn't want to go with them. The police said he was fighting them and trying to run away, but he needs a cane - how can someone who can hardly walk be trying to run? There were five officers and they threw him down on the ground. They took him off to their car.

I went inside and when I came back out, there were now about fifteen officers out there for one disabled guy. I don't know where they came from. There were four officers trying to get him into the car, dragging him and all of that.

I took a picture of them. I had a discussion with the officers.

I said, "People smoke for medication - it's better to have him sitting outside his door than to be off doing foolishness. There are more serious crimes out there to be fighting and look how many of you are here when there could be something serious happening elsewhere."

His mother came, and she showed them that he had one of those cards that allowed him to smoke for medical purposes. I don't know if they actually took him down to 31 Division but they had to let him go. The officers made it seem like such a big deal. That's why the community doesn't trust them.

One officer even wanted to take me on. He said that my mouth was too big, and another officer had to tell him to be quiet. I think I touched a nerve when I asked him, "Did you get bullied when you were younger?"

I told everyone to take out their cameras to try and calm it down. I said, "Take pictures! Take pictures!"

All the people were going click, click! That calmed down the police.

Being a minority you get a lot of different issues and a lot of different challenges that you have to face. You don't feel comfortable on a certain level. I mean, there are days that are beautiful - nobody's bothering you.

Why do we have all those officers patrolling the area? I know some people say it makes them feel safe, but do we need twenty police officers showing up for a misdemeanour?

◆

My opinion of Project Marvel?[2] That was great - the police had an operation, they completed the task that needed to be done and that was it. But the police come in here all the time harassing everybody. So you're harassing the wrong people - the good and the bad.

Kids are intimidated by seeing the police sometimes, because just watching their older brothers get harassed and beaten creates fear and dislike for police enforcement. Also, a lot of kids in the community don't have fathers because the men are in jail so they're growing up with their mothers. These kids already have these bad images of police officers in their minds.

◆

This happened when I was six or seven years old. There was a knock on the door of our apartment. I was too short to look through the peephole, so I asked who it was. The reply was that it was the police, and the man used an aggressive tone. I asked my mother to open the door.

The officer came in and pulled his gun on me. My mother stepped in and yelled at the officer, demanding to know what he was doing. She went outside the apartment with the officer. It was a noise complaint that came from someone downstairs. Maybe my brother was playing music too loud, but I don't remember.

Who pulls a gun on a kid for a noise complaint? I ran into the washroom, locked myself in and cried for two hours. I've been uncomfortable around police ever since.

Every time the police come around, it's always to try and intimidate somebody. Why can't they come around and try to get to know the community - build up a relationship? Come in to say hello and do your job to protect and make sure everything's okay.

Instead every time they come into the community, it's to act tough in their approach: "What are YOU doing here?" And you have to know that with the way you approach people, they're going to put up a resistance. Then the police forget their job and take it to a personal level.

It's like we don't want you here because you're not here to make sure we're okay and we're safe, you're coming here to harass people. Of course you'll get resistance from the people.

Better policing is something we need when looking towards the future. We need well trained officers - better trained. There's a dialogue that they should engage in - get to know who people are and they'll talk to you. Let them know you're just doing your job, then they'll accept you. There are a lot of issues that we have to face in Jane-Finch. I told the officers, "We would love to work with you guys, but we can't trust you."

I'm concerned that there are organizations and individuals who make it a point to instruct communities on their "legal rights" when it comes to dealing with police. Youth in high-priority areas are told it's their right not to identify themselves when a police officer asks them.

Well, the idea of "legal rights" sounds great up in the ivory towers, but the reality is far different. Go ahead and tell people to stand up for this right, but make sure you tell them it could come with a price. Tell them they may get charged (the police will think of something), or that this encounter could escalate into violence (and charges).

Yes, eventually your "legal rights" may kick in and you may have all charges dropped, but what about the cost of getting a lawyer? And what if you don't find a newspaper reporter willing to publicize your story? Do I need to remind people about the G20 in Toronto - people learned there how much "legal rights" helped them when the police directive was to lock people up now and sort it all out later.[3]

If you ask me, the smart advice is that when a police officer stops you, be respectful. Maybe you'll get respected back. If not, at least this is only a temporary annoyance. And if you can secretly turn on your cell or iPad to record the conversation, so much the better.

◆

In the past, the media portrayed Jane-Finch as an area with a lot of violence, a lot of drug dealing, a lot of players, so you've got those preconceptions about the area. So you've got these police coming in, maybe they're not trained the best, looking to see if they can make a bust and earn some stripes. They do not deal with these young men in the right way, so they ruin relationships that could have had potential. Instead, the people don't want to deal with the police at all. And it's all because they didn't come in with the right approach the first time. They've got to know how to talk to people.

◆

When police come in and they see guys running, the guys aren't running because they have drugs or guns on them; it's just that they don't want any dealings with the police. Police see people scatter and think it's because they're guilty of something. They can't be one-minded and think they're running because they're guilty. So you'll have police running after these people and they don't have anything.

◆

How can you help me raise my children? What can you do to help me? Why am I helping you? That's why if there's a crime or something, nobody says anything. Everyone keeps quiet.

They think, "Okay, if I help you, I'll put myself in jeopardy. What can you do to help me out of this situation? After I talk to you, I'm right back out there in the community and I'll have to deal with those people who probably know I said something."

So they'll hide it. They won't say much. Neighbourhood watch (chuckle) - I don't know about that. Everyone's tight-lipped when it comes to certain things.

◆

Police are watching these youth, ages ten to fourteen, because they don't want them to form gangs. This tactic of trying to scare the kids doesn't work. Do you know what they'll do? They'll hate the police. If something bad happens at their house, they won't talk to the police. They won't respect them, either.

◆

It is not right what the police do to the youth here. I don't like anything to do with the police here. If the police talk to the youth like human beings, if they respect them, and talk nice to them, the youth will be talking nice to them, too. It goes both ways to be respectful.

◆

I don't understand this - some of the police went through what the youth go through now. One officer told me the police stopped him when he was young. He said, "Do you think I like to stop kids? But I have to do my job."

I said, "Do your job right. Don't stop kids and scare them."

◆

You're so used to it, it's like, whatever. You never go up against the police or anybody in high places. It's your word against theirs.

"You have a voice" - you try to bring anything up, you get shut down. They don't listen. They just say and act like you've got a voice, that they're there to help you, they're there to protect and serve when all they do is bother people for no good reason. They'll stop you, ask you questions, see who you are, like these are things they don't have to do, but because they're in charge they feel that they can do anything.

I had an incident where I was having a conversation and then the police officer came. He was already saying that he was used to the situation. I was trying to say that the situation is different, I go to high school, and he said I go to the high school and I deal with this all the time. But he didn't hear my story, because he was already so used to it. So I just walked away because his mind is already set - "Oh, two girls fighting" - so his mind is set out as to he already knows what happened, that it's an altercation. But I didn't even know the female - I met her once in my life and then I met up with her again with that whole situation.

The officer already had his mind set, he knew what happened, but you don't come to a situation like that. You're a police officer: your mind should be open. You shouldn't be closed-minded, saying you've been through this already. He thought he already knew the whole story.

They need to go back to school again because they don't know how to do their job correctly. Of course they would handle it differently if it wasn't Jane and Finch. And he was a black officer. Black people that get a little power, they don't treat others with respect. They feel like they're better than people. Just because you're black, don't feel like you can treat me however. That's not correct. Then again, because they have a lot of power, they have to go and use it. At the end of the day, they'll misuse their power.

◆

We fear them because of the power they have over us. We always hear that if you're not doing anything, you shouldn't fear the police. They're doing their job, but the problem with that is they tend to cast a wide net.

Fishermen use a wide net because it grabs everything. That's how the police function here. When you tell the police what's happening, you might tell something that gets you caught in the wide net. That's why people can distrust the police. Once you bring the police in, they never leave. Some of them are rude and disrespectful. They love to play tag team - good cop, bad cop. It's an act to get what they want.

◆

I loved TAVIS. It was so different. For me, it was okay, for others it wasn't. People said that you're getting friendly with the police. Whatever happens, it impacts on all of us in the community. We want the bad element gone, but we're afraid to say anything. If the police beat on them, then they beat on us. Police say it's our fault because we don't talk. They don't understand that if we talk, we're the ones stuck smack in the middle.

When you have power, show respect. A smile doesn't kill. Police from our division said, we don't come here to meet and greet. We come here to do our jobs, as opposed to TAVIS. TAVIS would cushion the effect of the regular police. They smile and say good evening, they play with the kids. TAVIS would do their job in a milder way.

◆

When TAVIS first came, we talked to the TAVIS organizers and told them what we wanted, how to treat us, say hello and lower your voice even if you're angry. Half the guys who sell drugs don't live here. They drive in, stay the day, and drive out. They would sit in your doorway.

Some of the police need to be put in their place. My son and a friend were in the parking lot of our building. The police came over and asked what they were doing there. My son asked what right they had to stop him. When kids go outside and play in groups, let them be. Don't assume they're all drug dealers. The youth need to get outside and let off steam.

◆

The police will have their own problems and attitudes and bring them to the workplace. The police have the wrong impression of us. It's because of the attitude they have about Jane-Finch. They come here thinking we are all criminals. If it wasn't for the media, I guarantee police attitudes towards us would be different. Most of us are intelligent people, not criminals.

◆

They say Jane-Finch is bad, but I never lock my door. One night, we heard shots. We counted about six gun shots. Then we heard someone screaming. We found out the police were in the back. They were the ones shooting and running around out there. My mother went out, and the police yelled at her that they would charge her. They caught a guy. He was bleeding. They had him handcuffed. They kicked him, and punched him. They had him on the ground, one officer kneeled on him, and another was kicking him. There was a large white dog there, too.

Was it necessary to kick him while he was down and handcuffed already? Everybody came, and a woman was crying because she thought it was her son (it wasn't). It was so heart-wrenching. My daughter later heard that he was a troublemaker, dealing drugs and stuff.

◆

You don't want the police in your life at all. The police don't think about the impact they have. The next generation will be born and groomed to dislike the police. Their voice and their attitude reaffirms what the children have observed about police officers.

◆

You have a bunch of guys sitting around. They don't have jobs, so they sit and don't do anything. Maybe they smoke a bit, but they don't deal. But when the police come, they say don't run, but when they see police, they run.

The police will arrest you for no reason. You fear the possible consequences. It's a sense of powerlessness and it gets instilled into the next generation.

If the kids get arrested, you have to put up assets to bail them out, you take the time to bail them out, go to court, then the charges get tossed out because there was nothing there in the first place.

◆

It's not a matter of good or bad. We do need the police, but they have an attitude of power and right. That isn't helpful. We were told there is nothing we can do, so we have to adapt to them. The police won't meet us halfway.

When the police go out, what face do they show to the community? People remember the pain, not the good parts. If they hug you yesterday, but beat you tomorrow, you'll only remember the beating.

I meet some police who are willing to help, who will play with the kids. People ask why police stop us on the way to work, stop and ask us for ID. We would get a lot more crimes solved if not for the police attitude. Talk quietly and listen.

I've seen kids be rude to the police - they can't act like that. Police should understand and not lash out. You'll get to know the good officers from the bad ones, just by their attitude when they approach you.

Once they put your name in the system, it's not coming out. The police have the power to remove you from your life. Whether you're guilty or not, it gives you a sense of powerlessness.

You might call the police to help you, but you don't want the person removed. You might call to make the beating stop, but the police will come and make the situation worse.

We create monsters out of the police to scare our kids, but that turns against us. The experience the kids have with police and jail makes them worse. I knew who someone got sent to a mental health centre after she was arrested. I thought she would finally be treated and get the help she needed. Instead, she absorbed all the negative traits from the drug dealers and violent people who were also there.

◆

When it comes to police, I think we need more accountability. Don't get me wrong, I think there are a lot of good people wearing police uniforms. And to be fair, policing is not the easiest job around.

At the same time, there are officers who make the force look bad through their actions and attitudes. There should be a way to get them as far away from the public as possible. If I work at a fast food place and I screw up, maybe someone's burger gets burned. If I'm a police officer and I screw up, lives can be affected, ruined, or ended. I know this can be a heavy responsibility.

That being said, those who aren't willing or able to shoulder that responsibility professionally shouldn't be there. It's not like they aren't being paid well for it.[4]

◆

For the complaining that does goes on here about the police, I don't think people realize how privileged we are that we can criticize the police. You can go to some parts of the world where you can't even think of negative things, you can't even look at their side of the street because they might arrest you or shoot you on the spot. We don't understand how lucky we are that we can meet in groups where we talk about holding police or politicians accountable. In many parts of the world you can't do that at all.

Notes

[1] From http://www.torontopolice.on.ca/tavis/: "The Toronto Anti-Violence Intervention Strategy (TAVIS) is an intensive, violence reduction and community mobilization strategy intended to reduce crime and increase safety in our neighbourhoods."

"TAVIS is led by the Toronto Police Service. Partners include Toronto Community Housing and City of Toronto departments such as Parks, Forestry and Recreation, Toronto Public Health, Social Development, Finance and Administration, Toronto Office of Partnerships and others."

"An essential part of TAVIS is engagement with community members. It becomes the support system necessary to deal more effectively with the root causes of crime. The success of TAVIS is not based on the number of arrests made but on the reduction in crime, enhancement of public trust and confidence, and the building of relationships within the communities most affected by violence."

2 On Tuesday December 13, 2011, a joint-forces initiative culminated in a series of raids across Canada. Police executed sixty-seven search warrants simultaneously in Toronto, London, Hamilton, Durham Region, York Region, Peel Region, Windsor, Ottawa, Calgary (Alberta), and Surrey (B.C.). It started in May 2013 after police determined that a number of shootings in the Jane-Driftwood area were gang-related. Two gangs operated on opposing sides of Jane Street, one located on Driftwood Avenue (east of Jane) and the other on Gosford Boulevard (west of Jane). The operation was code-named "Project Marvel" because gang members used the names of Marvel Comics super heroes. As of Thursday, December 15th, 2011, "Project Marvel" resulted in 396 adult charges and 84 young offender charges. Police seized $110,000, 27 firearms, 2.75 kilograms of cocaine, 332 grams of marijuana and 32 grams of MDMA, the main component of ecstasy.

3 In June 2010, there was a summit of the leaders of G20 nations held in Toronto. It was marked by a number of protests, one of which turned into a riot (June 26). There were over 1,100 arrests made over the course of the protests and nearly 800 of those arrested were released without charge.

4 "New deal makes Toronto police highest paid in country," *Toronto Star*, 05 May 2011. From the article: "A first-class constable earning $81,249 in 2010 will make $90,623 in 2014 ... The net $905.9 million police operating budget is the largest single item on the city budget. Salaries, benefits and overtime account for nearly 90 per cent of it."

My Story - Six (Female)

"You never know where life is going to take you."

Back in Jamaica, I lived at the bottom of a hill located in the foothills of the Blue Mountains. It was a cash crop farm where we planted food like yam potatoes and pigeon peas.

By the time we grew up, our grandparents were farming the land. My father had to work as a gardener because the farm could not support us. There were bushes everywhere, and we had bananas, grapefruit, and akees.

As I said, we lived at the bottom of the hill - two more houses were located on the top of the hill. The driveway didn't go down to our house. It still needs to be finished.

When my father got sick in 2010, the car that came to get him stopped at the first house. He was too weak to walk, so we used a wheel barrow to take him up to that car. Some people have died because no one could reach them in time. There are items I would have liked to send back home, but they couldn't be delivered to the door.

I never had a childhood because I had to watch my brothers and sisters. Some days, there was no food left for me. I was running the house since I was fourteen, because my mom also had to work. She was a seamstress, but they didn't pay her enough, so she worked as a housekeeper. My dad worked for about four pounds a week.

That's how I learned to budget because he'd give me the money to take care of the kids. I'd go to the bushes and look for things to cook. I'd go to school, cook, and look after the children. I had to wash clothes for six kids. If I made a mistake and the money was gone before the end of the week, we'd have to figure out what to do. My step father hated credit.

Cornmeal was the cheapest food you could buy. Back then cornmeal was for the dogs. Sometimes when the money ran out, I could only afford cornmeal. We'd eat cornmeal with pumpkin, cornmeal with peas, cornmeal with cabbage (we planted cabbage in our garden), and cornmeal with callaloo. I'd pick the vegetables and I'd cook them. I was so ashamed that we ate cornmeal; I didn't want anyone to know.

So now it turns out that cornmeal is one of the best foods you can eat. Even though we were ashamed, we were eating the best food nutritionally. That's why my family was so strong.

When times got tough in the 1970s, everyone ate cornmeal. It got so that there wasn't any left for the dogs!

We always had rice and peas for Sunday dinner. That was always the big meal of the week and a tradition in Jamaica. That might be the only good meal you got some weeks.

My sisters brought their boyfriends to meet me because I was running the house. These boys didn't believe that I was the oldest sister. When I was nineteen, I looked like a twelve year old.

I grew up in a mixed family. We're Asian, white, and Jamaican (descendants of the Maroons). My great grandmother was Japanese and married a Scottish man she met in Panama.

My grandmother, who was Scottish and Japanese, married a bi-racial man (French Maroon and Irish) and her father kicked her out of the house and said her name was not to be mentioned around the house ever again. This was because she married a mulatto.

There were racists in Jamaica. My sister has red hair and fair skin. At our school which was mostly black, she was called "red Mongoose." We weren't allowed to speak Patois at home. If we did, we were beaten and told to speak English.

I spoke with an English accent. One day I was stoned by construction workers. They wondered why I spoke English, and they called me "Chocolate." I learned Patois when I came to Canada. I came here speaking with an English accent.

In Jamaica, I worked with a rich family as a nanny and as a pastry cook. These people were the ones who were influential in my coming to Canada. The idea was that I would join them in Miami.

That didn't work out. I did not come to Canada with the intention of staying. Initially, I only came because I didn't have an American visa and was going to stay here until I got one. Instead, I got my Canadian citizenship in 2003. My relative called from the States and said I could apply for my Green Card, but I said I loved Canada.

I came over August 6, 1988, and I had no idea where I was going. I knew my friends lived here, but not what part of Canada. My foster mother lived here in a building on Driftwood Avenue. She came here to work as a nanny.

I first lived in Etobicoke, but soon left and rented a room in the very building where I'm living now. In 1994 I went back to Etobicoke for four years because I didn't like it here. I liked Etobicoke because that was where I lived first.

I lived with a woman for the entire four years because I couldn't find a place of my own that I could afford in the area. It was very expensive at the time. I wasn't working full-time on a regular basis. The woman's niece was coming, so I had to leave and return to Jane-Finch. I ended up renting a room in the same building I had left in 1994, and got my own apartment in 2009.

In one way or another, I've been living in Jane-Finch and this particular building for twenty years. During that time, I've noticed a lot of the Italians have moved out to Woodbridge, and many of their homes have been bought by Vietnamese. They're very nice people, but so many can't speak English so we can't get them involved and joining programs because of the language barrier.

Because of my experience back home, I wanted to study restaurant management here. But I wasn't allowed to take it because it was deemed that I would take a job away from Canadians.

So I went to Humber College for Early Childhood Education (1990-1992). It was a two year course, but I didn't like my placement, so I dropped the course and switched to Gerontology Activation at Humber College. This was a very specialized field of study that would teach you how to design therapeutic programs for older adults.

I got a job as a home support worker in 1993, but continued to take the courses at night and graduated from Humber in 2000. I am trained as a Personal Support Worker (Ontario). I did a Bridge and in January 2004 I got my National Certificate. I'm also trained in Basic Youth Counselling, and still look for ways to use those skills.

The TTC accident completely changed my life. In October 2004, I fell off a bus and damaged my knee. This accident finished my career because I was unable to work. My job was everything to me. I got depressed and the 2005 Summer Of The Gun added to my stress.[1]

Somehow, I wanted to get involved and help the young men and help stop the killing. I joined ACORN in 2005 and became a co-chair of the local chapter. I found that getting involved really helped me a lot.

The accident caused me to lose every cent I had. Things got so bad that I was on welfare for a year. My case against the TTC was finally settled in July 2011. In October 2011, once again I fell on a bus and this time I damaged my shoulder. Despite chronic pain, I am determined to continues my volunteer work to this day.

I took a class at Black Creek Pioneer Village in silk screening. I took it with the intention to start a business because I needed to make money after the accident. You can buy plain white scarves for under three dollars each. Take a basin and mix alum in it. You can add colour to the alum. Let the mixture stay overnight. The starch is thick enough that you can draw pictures in it. These scarves can be sold for a lot of money. I made six scarves and gave five away as gifts.

I became an Avon lady but gave up after a month. Everybody was selling Avon products in my building.

I also sold Parklane jewellery for a time.

Then I went to Legal Shield because they paid more in commissions. The problem is that it's difficult to get people to sign up. It's a prepaid legal service where you pay a monthly fee and get a discount on legal services. I wish I had it when I had my accident because it would have helped with my legal costs. You get your will and power of attorney free when you sign up. You don't have to buy inventory and you get a commission for every sale plus residuals.

In 1999, I spent six months in Louisville, Kentucky. I was asked to go there by a woman who knew my work from Jamaica. I would go into homes and arrange the furniture, clean the cupboards, and everything else that was necessary. This was something I would do even if the house wasn't going up for sale.

I also would make sure that expensive stuff wasn't being thrown out because the owners didn't know the value of the items. I know a lot about antiques. Looking back, it turns out I was decluttering before it got that fancy name. Now I see people charging hundreds and hundreds of dollars for what I was doing back then. I have a knack for that kind of work. I like putting things in order.

When I was a support worker, I worked in palliative care. This would allow a person to die at home with their loved ones present. In America, if you have the money, they'll keep you alive for donkey's years. Those tubes hurt. It's outright cold and disgusting. It's a bad thing.

In Canada, they say everything's covered, but it's not. One time I was working with a client who had leukaemia. She went into remission twice. The third time, she was denied the drugs she needed to keep her comfortable because it wasn't viable, because she was dying. They used very pretty words to cover what they were doing to save money. Eventually she died. You won't hear health people talk about it.

It was twenty-four hour care. During daytime, I did regular work, bathing people, providing relief for family members (let them leave the house and get a break), things we called Activities of Daily Living.

I worked from 11 p.m. to eight in the morning, and then did my day job for the same company. It was a thirteen hour day. I worked a lot of overtime but the government took most of it in taxes. Because I was single, I had less deductions.

When I came to Canada, the first church I entered had female deacons. Seeing women give communion was a really bad culture shock for me. I was only the second black person in the church that I'm in now. It's become much more multicultural since then. They are nice people. They took me to appointments when I broke my foot. They even helped me pay the rent when I was on welfare.

Not too many black people will stay with the church. That's probably due to how the service is set up. It's kind of dull. Everything is so reverential. Everything is mostly read during the service. The African church service is more hands on.

I've always been an activist. I knew about the plight of native Canadians before I came to Canada. I stood up for the natives and people got angry with me. They asked why I would care. You do to a people what was done to natives, you'll find they have a lot of problems. And whose fault is that?

I worked as a nanny for the family of a man who lived in Etobicoke, and he called me "the little black woman." I paid him no mind and he came to like me. I had leave and was asked to go in and clean. I saw there was a white woman there. He called her in to take my place. She couldn't even clean. I saw this and didn't go back after that.

Canada is racist, but it's hidden. They're sneaky about it. In the U.S., they tell you straight to your face. It's changed drastically in Canada since I came here. There was a time, if you rented a place owned by white people, if they saw your face, they wouldn't rent to you. They'd tell you something had come up, and so they were giving the place to a relative.

At my job as a support worker, clients would tell my employer not to send over any black people - this was in the 1990s!

My brother was driving on a trip and almost got locked up in a small U.S. town. The sheriff pulled him over and was looking for something. They still call you "boy" and "n****r." My brother was so scared that he drove all the way to Florida without stopping at any more towns. In Canada, they won't beat you, call you "n****r" and lock you up.

The welfare system here is racist. They treat blacks differently from whites - they say we're lazy, don't want to work, come here to live off the government. It's different now because the staff are better trained. They have no choice, as people would complain and go to lawyers.

When my welfare was running out, I was looking for where I could get help. The black woman who dealt with me was very nasty. She made me feel very small. I think she resented how others had treated her as a black woman and she was taking it out on me. A white woman came to help me and treated me nicely. All the same, I will never go on welfare again.

I've been very involved politically. In the 2006 municipal campaign, I helped ACORN as they worked on the Anthony Perruzza campaign for

Councillor in Ward 8. I was attracted by the campaign promise to introduce Landlord Licensing.

My building (located on Jane Street) had numerous violations. Inspectors were called and made the landlords fix everything. Things get done if you fight for them.

I stayed out of the 2010 municipal election because I worked on a "get out the vote" campaign and needed to be neutral. I will not join any political party. People in the area say they want change, but then vote for the same party that is always in power here. They don't care about their own interests.

I am frustrated about the inability to get things done in Jane-Finch. We try to do things but get blocked. Agencies block residents and volunteers because they will lose jobs if we can succeed in making improvements. We need to take more control over our community. Others get the jobs in our area.

You have to weigh the good and the bad in people.

Black males get singled out and they need to realize this and not get into trouble - it's worse for them. They need adult supervision and guidance. They have no male models. They need someone to tell them they can do better. Others stay away from these youth, but I won't let fear stop me from helping these boys. Who is watching these children? Who is giving them hope? Let our boys know they matter, and that someone cares about them.

When people ask me how I got here, I tell them God brought me here. When God is on your side, and you trust in Him, everything works out for the best. By all rights, I should not have come to Canada, much less live here in my own place. Over the twenty-odd years since I packed up my things and left my native land, I have endured a lot.

I tried to leave Jane-Finch, but could not get a place in Etobicoke. I came here on a medical certificate. Every year you had to renew the visa and get a permit to work in this country. I was supposed to get my landed status three years after I came here, but I couldn't.

Finally, I asked Ottawa why I was not getting my papers. When I first got here, I had chest pains and the government thought I was going to be a burden on the medical system. So the man gave me a medical pass that said I would be tested and if I had heart trouble, they would send me back home. This is why I didn't get my papers. I was sent to get my heart checked, and it turned out it wasn't my heart. I was born with a hole that caused really bad acid reflux - I think it's called Buerger's disease. So I got my papers after all.

If I hadn't passed the heart test, if I had found a place in Etobicoke, I would not have been here to go to the community forum and become a member of Jane-Finch On The Move. As for my accident, it was a blessing and a curse. Normally, I would have worked Saturdays, which is when the forum was held. If it wasn't for the accident, I wouldn't have joined ACORN, nor Jane-Finch On The Move, nor met all the people I have these past years. You just never know how life will turn out.

Notes

[1] For Toronto residents and media, 2005 has been called both "The Year of the Gun" and "The Summer of the Gun," due to the record number of shooting deaths. Fifty-five people died in a year that saw two hundred and thirty-two shooting incidents, with one hundred and ninety-six people shot. (Figures from http://www.canadafreepress.com/gun-shootings-toronto-2005.htm) If one wants to use the technical definition of summer (June 21 to September 21), twenty-four people were shot and killed that summer. Interestingly enough, the RCMP made the following comment on its web site regarding 2005's gun violence: "most of the gun-related homicides occur in at-risk neighbourhoods such as the Jane-Finch area," and did not mention any other location (http://www.rcmp-grc.gc.ca/pubs/yg-ja/toronto20-eng.htm).

There were seven gun-related deaths that took place in and around the Jane-Finch area in 2005. Here is a list of names and known details so that these victims can be seen as more than just numbers (basic information from http://torontowiki.org/Summer_of_The_Gun):

April 24: Livette Olivea Miller, 26, a single mother of four, was shot to death at the Prestige Palace Nightclub at 9 Milvan Drive, just off Finch Avenue West (and west of Highway 400). Six men were injured.

June 24: Jason Thomas Joseph, 26, was shot to death by two men on bicycles on a public walkway at 79 Gosford Boulevard. Two other men were wounded. Police believe the killing was a case of mistaken identity.

August 30: Jason Huxtable, 18, was shot to death inside a parked car on Magellan Drive, south of 1901 Sheppard Avenue West. A fifteen year old boy was charged with second-degree murder.

September 10: Andre Malik Burnett, 24, was shot to death on a footbridge that crosses Driftwood Avenue, only a few hundred metres away from Jane Street. On May 17, he had been released after nearly 22 months in custody. (http://www.ottawamenscentre.com/news/20050620_case_closed.htm)

September 13: Sureshkumar Kanagaratnam, 28, was gunned down in the parking lot of the Yorkwoods Plaza at 2857 Jane Street. He had worked as a tool and die maker for the past seven years. He was at the plaza to get dinner.

December 1: part-time used-car salesperson Sepehr (Danny) Fatulahzadeh-Rabti, 25, was shot to death by two men after a fight at his family's car lot at 4877 Steeles Avenue West. Two men would enter guilty pleas in 2008.

On Dec. 23, Cordell Charles Skinner, 25, was gunned down on the grounds of 5 Turf Grassway. This happened near a daycare centre as parents were picking up their children. No one else was hurt.

The gun-related numbers would drop slightly in 2006 with one hundred and eighty-nine shooting incidents, one hundred and sixty-six people shot, and forty-one people killed. 2007 saw a new record with sixty-six gun deaths. The Jane-Finch community was rocked by two shooting deaths, the May 23 murder of fifteen year old Jordan Manners at C. W. Jefferys Collegiate Institute, and the July 22 death of eleven year old Ephraim Brown, killed when shot in the neck by a stray bullet. The numbers dropped noticeably in 2008, with one hundred twenty-six shooting incidents, one hundred and forty-two people shot, and thirty-one killed. 2013 saw a further decline with twenty-two shooting deaths. (Figures from http://www.canadafreepress.com/gun-shootings-toronto.htm and http://www.torontopolice.on.ca/statistics/ytd_stats.php)

Relationships

Love makes the world go round. Doesn't it?

Sometimes a woman needs a man. Someone to be your partner and be there when your world is falling apart. But most men don't understand. When I go to school or go to work, I still have to come home, cook, clean up the house, do the laundry.

◆

I've got two kids, and I don't want a man. I balance it out: if I get a man, I get problems.

◆

I've always been a straight forward individual - I say what I want and I say what I feel so I've never had anyone take advantage of my kindness. I've been able to keep long-lasting relationships just because I'm a people person. We experiment when we're younger because we don't have as much knowledge, and experience leads to wisdom. Hopefully, you catch on quick enough to not make the same mistake ten thousand times.

I've been married for eight years now, and every relationship has its ups and downs. At the end of the day, it's discipline, giving and taking, and I know it's not easy for two individuals from different walks of life to join together and make things work. It's got to rain sometime in every relationship - it's all about how you get through the storm.

If you have enough determination, it can be done. We may come to the table sometimes with a little baggage, but if you have someone who truly cares about you, then they'll help you get through those things until it gets better. It always gets better - at least I hope so.

◆

Men want you to mind them. I ask them, what are you bringing to the table? I'm working, I'm a professional, but they want to tell me what to do with my life. They don't want to help you. I'm not going to mind him. He's supposed to take care of me or at least not sit around all day, especially if I'm working too. Now, I look after myself. I dumped one man because he wouldn't stay loyal to me. If you're going to have me, you have to have me alone.

◆

Relationships can last. Both of you have to understand that you might argue five minutes from now, but you have to find a conclusion to work that out. You communicate and talk about those things. Sometimes in an argument, we take things to heart when it's just an argument - you're just frustrated at that time and the other person should understand that you're just frustrated and saying things you don't mean. Don't take it so personally.

A lot of relationships break up because of what that person said at the moment. If you were friends, you could understand that the other was upset and didn't really mean it, but who else can you take your frustrations out on?

I feel that if you can have that level of communication, nothing could break the bond and that relationship would last. I know sometimes you might be miserable but I also know at the end of the day, I love you and you love me. You might have those days where I have to be understanding. This is the person you have to cry with, laugh with, share your secrets with, the person that can tell you that you're doing something wrong and not get upset because you know they're trying to help you and are seeing things you're not seeing. It's not a one person relationship, it's two, there's rights and wrongs, and you're not there to judge, you're there to empathize.

◆

In every relationship, there are signals and flashing lights that should be paid attention because they pave the way for other things. Sometimes a person is infatuated, the chemicals are rushing, and the person turns a blind eye. Personally, I chose not to have children early, not even in my marriage because I wanted to see how things were going to work. I didn't want to become a woman forced to raise a child all by herself.

So I took it slow when it came to children. I even told the man I married that I didn't want to raise a child by myself. He was respectful of that. We waited for seven years and then it was time. I made up my mind to take that step, and I'm happy I did.

◆

I was born in Canada, but after I got my high school diploma, my family decided to stay in Egypt for a few years. I met a young man there that I fell in love with and wanted to marry. My parents didn't agree, but I did insist on it happening, no matter what the circumstances, and I did eventually marry him.

When my parents and I returned to Canada, I started the process to bring him here. He came a year later. The problems between me and him eventually started happening. He didn't like Canada while I loved Canada.

We stayed together for seven years. I wanted to have kids with him because I knew he was the one man I fell in love with. I couldn't seem to get pregnant. It was one disappointment after another. I lost all hope in having kids. It just wasn't happening.

I finally got the nerve to go to a doctor and see if I had a problem. The results were that I could indeed get pregnant. All the problems we had with no pregnancy, him not liking Canada, and him being away from his family led us to get a divorce. It was a tough decision for us.

He went back to Egypt to be with all his friends and family. He got married to another woman and had a baby girl. I later noticed that my heart wouldn't let me go on with my life without him being there every step of the way. I went to Egypt so I could marry him again. We had a lot of problems with his wife getting jealous and yelling at me and him for going through the marriage even though he was still married to her. She never stopped calling me on the phone and insulting me. I took all the pain and verbal abuse because I was in love with him.

I still hope to get pregnant with him; that would be a great accomplishment for me. My heart gets torn more and more each day because of the hardships with the pregnancy and the other woman he married. I'm always travelling back and forth from Canada to Egypt - it's like having to choose between my family and my husband. My heart breaks in half each time. I'm not happy at all. I hope that one day I can get out of this situation.

◆

Wisdom comes with age. When you're younger, you're not thinking the way you think now. It takes time for you to grow. I think relationships are often rushed. People don't take the time to get to know each other.

Developing friendship is a big part of relationships, and I feel that if a lot of people start off as friends and get to grow and then decide to try a relationship, it might work out in their best interests.

There are different sectors in relationships, I think. You might want a relationship where you're just seeing a person, you're not seeing a future with them, this is for the moment. But that's not the understanding of the other person, as they're thinking on a different level. So I guess it's communication and talking to make sure you're on the same page, to make sure that you're not guessing or hoping for something that's not going to happen.

Then when it doesn't happen, you try to blame the other person while you could have easily fixed that if you had just communicated with each other.

◆

I don't like men because they're always trying to trick me. When I was fifteen, there was a boy that went to school with me. One day, he told me my stepfather had left some bananas for me to pick up. So when I went to get the bananas, he grabbed on to me. My mother taught us to fight when a guy tried to rape us. So I hit him with my elbow and kicked him in the groin. Then I ran away.

◆

It's good to know what you want, but if you go into a relationship with expectations, then you'll disappoint yourself because you'll want to change this person into what you want them to be, when that's not really who they are. You'll spend all your time and energy changing this person and then you lose your own identity. Or you might change yourself to suit that person.

◆

I punished every man for what happened to me with men when I was younger.

◆

When it comes to relationships, I'm a dreamer. I try to find the best in a person and hope that I can change them to the way that I want them, or that they'll eventually grow up. I used to ignore a lot of signs that were given to me in relationships, but I would also learn from each relationship. Every relationship is always different.

They say opposites attract so we have this picture in our minds of what we think we want, and then your true love can be the complete opposite of those expectations that you had. And maybe there's a tendency to over think that picture, and create an image that eliminates so many good potential partners. Sometimes people look for someone who will make them stand out, so they create this image of a perfect person that they want. You have to be realistic.

Going back to saying opposites attract, it could be that one person has a strength that is your weakness. So you acknowledge that and make it work for both of you. People can have complementary qualities that bring balance into a relationship.

◆

One thing I didn't really notice until I got to post-secondary schooling and left the safety of this community, is that I felt a sort of reluctance to tell people I was from Jane-Finch.

Once I went to university and started interacting with people who were from different social classes, mainly higher social classes, I didn't really want to tell people. Not to say that I was embarrassed; instead, I felt stigmatized. And this was the first time in my life I felt this way.

I was meeting people who came from places like Bayview and other upper class neighbourhoods. Now I didn't have the safety of my peers, people who were living the same reality as myself. For example, I didn't have a car, and now I see the other males who have a car. I wouldn't call myself an old-fashioned type of man, but I don't want to date a girl and have her drive me. That's just not how it is. Even if it is her car, I'd have to drive it myself.

In the context of my community, it's really funny how I internalized it in my relationships when I started to deal with people from outside. You worry about their perceptions, whether they'll think less of you. And usually I don't care about that kind of stuff, but when it comes to relationships, it's different. Sometimes I'd say I was from Jane and Steeles because I do live somewhat in the centre of those intersections.

At the same time, you do have women who think it's barbaric and they're turned on. It's like the geographic equivalent of "jungle fever." The problem is that they frame you as being this thug or animal, someone who is dangerous.

Three summers ago, one of my closest friends participated in a government exchange program to learn French as a second language. He lives just off Driftwood Avenue and he ended up going to Sudbury for four weeks to take part in this program. There were people from all across the country, from different universities, such as University of British Columbia and University of Alberta.

He was asked where he lived and when he finally broke it down to Jane and Finch, he said the level of interest he got from girls was ridiculous. Some girls said they did case studies on people living in Jane-Finch. They found him so exotic that he got lucky with five of the girls attending that program.

◆

It's good to look at a relationship as a friendship. I think when some people get into a relationship, they think "Okay, now we're dating," and they forget about the friendship when they were able to talk and share, enjoy a movie and do the things that actually count.

Instead, now they focus on being "together" and here comes the limitations and the judgments. All those things make you feel suffocated, like you can't fully express yourself, and you lose the communication.

◆

No young girl was safe where I was growing up in Jamaica. My cousin called me to go behind the shop. He had something for me, but I had to go get it there. I knew he wanted to interfere with me. If you wanted to give me something, give it to me over the counter. If I didn't know how to fight, I would have been raped so many times.

◆

Courting is very important: go to movies, go to dinner, and you do that for a few months. Relationships get rushed far too quickly, people try to get together on the first date, push it to the next level, and things can tumble from there. You should nurture a relationship.

Courting is where you can learn about the other person, try to learn about their character before things get too far. You may learn that you don't like that person's attitude, or that they're too aggressive. Instead, relationships move so quickly that you miss all that. And when you do find out, it becomes a matter of "well, I've been with this person for so long, and I've done all this with this person, so I can't be bothered to go through it all over again with someone new."

If you gave it time, maybe you could see that particular character trait and realize that it's something you've seen before and didn't like. If there was communication in this relationship, you could talk about it and see if the person could work on it.

◆

Now that I'm in my thirties, I know what I want. It took me a while to figure that out. Now I can tell myself that I don't need a guy that can't do anything for me, who is not spiritual like me, who isn't someone I can talk to, or only comes over at night time - I don't need that kind of guy, I'm worth more than that. I know what to look for, and I know that there are a lot of men in this world. Sometimes, we forget that, and if we get one man, we try so hard to hold on to him because we think there's a man shortage.

Women work off their emotions, they get more involved, and put more into the relationship. Before they know it, they've already given so much of their emotions and it's too late to just turn back.

◆

All in all, I've been able to build a nice thick wall around me to keep others at a distance. Sometimes, I do miss having someone close, but I don't feel that way very often. Like I said, I built a good wall. It helps that none of my relationships were much fun after the early part. The biggest problem is that whoever I was with would find a big list of things wrong with me.

Some of the flaws were common (my bad), and maybe I could work on them, but what really annoyed me is how each potential partner candidate would find a whole new pile of imperfections with me. So generally, I'd be the one to end things. The way I see it, if there are so many things that you want to change about me, what exactly is there that you like about me? Better to end it so you can find someone closer to your ideal. If I'm a Hyundai Accent and you really have your heart set on a Cadillac, we're both better off if you go visit a Cadillac dealer.

◆

This is something a few of us have been discussing; namely, are relationships different inside Jane-Finch as opposed to elsewhere?

The Jane-Finch area has a lot of subsidized housing, and who lives in this housing? Single mothers. At least that's the way the area is portrayed, that there are a lot of single mothers, a lot of baby mothers, a lot of one parent homes. It's a stigma and one that continues from one generation to the next. A lot of people grow up seeing that and thinking it's okay. Why does this happen?

Some of it might be financial. When you don't have much money, and can't afford your own place, you could rush into a relationship just so you have a place to stay. Single mothers could use a man in their life. The relationship doesn't work out, and the woman blames herself.

It's an economic issue in certain areas. And in an area like Jane-Finch where people have that view that there's a lot of single mothers and there's a lot of housing complexes, no one's going to believe that any true relationships can exist in an area like this. And if there is such a relationship, people will wonder about it, saying that's not the way it's supposed to be.

If a guy tries to pick you up, he automatically thinks you're single and if you say you're married, he's thinking, "Really? Are you just saying that because you don't want to talk to me?" If you live in Richmond Hill, they'll be more accepting of your relationship status. But if you say that here, you're met with disbelief. The assumption is that relationships in Jane-Finch can never be a happy story. It feels like there are so many barriers here to having healthy relationships.

Of course, there are households where there is a man in the picture, but if they're known to be in the picture, if they're put on the record, then the rent goes up. I'm sure this affects the relationship in one way or another. There's no growth in that relationship.

It's one thing if you're both living there in housing to save up and one day move away together. Instead, many times, the male figures in these situations are temporary. They're there for maybe a year, and then they move on. And there are single mothers who are in housing because they feel safe. They think if they have kids, it'll be easier for them to get housing or at least that's where their social worker will refer them. So they'll be living in subsidized housing and there will not be a male figure in the picture. And that's why they're on assistance. Only there really is a male figure present, he's just staying low and being that convenient. He's chipping in and chipping out.

If the father's not in the picture, if he's not on the birth certificate, then he's not paying support. If there is a man, you have to hide him. Then people don't see the mother and father roles. The guy comes at night or when no one's looking. No one sees them together.

If you meet someone who's potential husband material, someone you can start a future with, and you want to bring him home, well you can only have a visitor for nine days out of the month. Those are the rules in housing. If you want to build together, grow a relationship, you have to be kind of shady about it. If people see this individual staying at your house or see him coming and going, they'll think he's not supposed to be there. God forbid that any of these people know the super. You have to be careful how you conduct yourself.

It affects so many things. The children need proper parenting, and single mothers don't want to make these men known to the children until they're sure about the relationship. What kind of models are children seeing? If they're raised in an environment where men are in the shadows, they could see this as being acceptable, boys and girls alike. The whole idea of men sticking to the shadows sounds like they're some kind of love ninjas.

I think these "love ninjas" are afraid of the responsibility. In my opinion, these men are cowards but you can't blame them because most likely it's what they saw while growing up.

If a guy looks like he's potentially a good man, there are other women who'll want him too. Now it's drama. You can come out your door with popcorn, sit down and watch the show. Relationships are a big thing in Jane-Finch. That's what most of the dramas are about: it's some man or some woman, who slept with who, and it's out there for everyone to hear. It's always something, and so you never really see a good relationship being mentioned out there. Instead, it's always drama.

My Story - Seven (Male)

"I enjoy being the way I am."

Most of the time I'm here in Jane-Finch. I enjoy traveling around the area, walking around, passing by. I enjoy seeing familiar faces, like people I knew from my high school.

I enjoy where I live right now, and I've lived here since the summer of 1997. I was seventeen when we moved. Before that, I used to live on Grandravine Drive, between Jane Street and Driftwood Avenue.

It's just me and my mom now. My dad lives with my step family. My family's Jamaican, and my dad's American. My dad enjoys living here in Canada. He came over a long time ago. I was born here.

I enjoy being single. You can be by yourself and have your privacy. If things don't turn out, you can just go away and then come back some other time.

I enjoy going to the program that's given by the Jane/Finch Family and Community Centre. It's called "Getting In Touch."[1]

During the day, if there's nothing going on at my community program, I help out my mother. I do chores, I go buy groceries. I enjoy cooking. I cook pancakes, French toast, eggs, rice, French fries - I slice the potatoes and I cook them. I also bake cakes and I can bake chicken. Sometimes I read story books and story bibles. I'll read newsletters I got from my summer job. In my free time, I like to draw. When I was in high school, we used to draw a lot.

I like being physically active, healthy, and being in shape. I watch my blood sugar and watch my diet. I don't want to get diabetes. I enjoy eating things I like, including some sweets, so I don't want anything to happen to me where I can't eat this and I can't eat that. I know folks who are diabetic. I enjoy being the way I am, not getting sick, not getting injured. A long time ago, I used to have headaches and I had stomach pains but I've never been seriously sick. I had fluid on my knee once and I was at the hospital for that.

I enjoy doing important stuff like going to meetings for my community programs. I enjoy going to community meetings, rallies and marches. I've played basketball, volleyball, floor hockey, soccer, baseball. I still play volleyball at the Driftwood Community Centre.

I get scared when I hear about shootings. I usually don't get into trouble. I feel okay when I'm going to Jane and Finch and there's nothing happening. Good thing I wasn't there when I heard about a shooting going on.

Once I saw a dead body on the ground. I wasn't sure if it was a guy or a girl. This was right over by the townhouses near Gosford Public School where the parking lot is. I went since everyone was there watching and seeing what was going on. It made me feel scared.

I'd like to stop the shooting, make the area safer for everyone. I saw a girl get hit by a bus once, just over by Driftwood Avenue at the lights. I saw people get arrested before, right in front of my building. I've heard people get into arguments. I might argue back if they start arguing at me.

Whenever I get a pay check, I like to make sure I pay my income tax. I want to get everything done and out of the way so that I don't have to worry about it later. I don't want to end up like Wesley Snipes.[2]

I'd like to meet politicians and ask them how they run stuff, how they hire people, how they enjoy being in charge. I'd like to get ideas from them. I enjoy seeing them at festivals. I've never voted because I'm afraid of being on a losing team. I'm shy to vote by myself.

Notes

[1] Getting In Touch: "This is a community mental health social/recreational drop-in program for adults. A safe environment is provided to enable learning and to provide support in times of crisis, change, loneliness and isolation."

"Group activities include a weekly community kitchen, monthly celebrity cook visits, physical exercises, cultural sharing, games, educational workshops, life skills, bingo, crafts, outings and more. All group activities are planned with and by the participants at monthly business meetings and respond to the interests and requests of the members."

"The program space is accessible and the program provides TTC, childcare and light refreshments."
http://janefinchcentre.org/community-programs/community-mental-health

[2] On February 1, 2008, actor Wesley Snipes was found guilty of failing to file U.S. federal income tax returns, and was sentenced to three years in prison.

Politics

Pondering people, politicians, and protest.

Politicians are only nice to us when they want our vote. They are useless, all of them. I knew one politician, whenever he would see me, he would say to me, "Oh, are you going to vote for me, will you volunteer for me?," and now when he sees me, he doesn't say hello. He lost the election, but it's not my fault he lost.

◆

It bothers me when people say that government should be run like a business. In theory I agree, but only if we mean that government should be run like a successful business. Instead, it seems that too many people who say this (often politicians) equate "running a business" with "cutting costs." And that's it. Pull out the scissors and cut, cut, cut.

I can't think of many businesses that have been successful in the long-term with a strategy based on cutting costs. There's nothing wrong with cutting fat. There's definitely nothing wrong with becoming more efficient. However, once the scissors become the prime strategy, eventually it's muscle and vital organs that get cut. Successful businesses invest wisely in their companies. That's what governments should do.

Look at where spending money gets the biggest result. What helps communities grow? What kind of programs keep people healthy and inspires them to succeed? I'm all for cutting wasteful spending, but who gets to decide what is wasteful?

When someone insists on cutting money from social programs now when the end result is that we'll spend more money on jails later, that person is either a short-sighted simpleton or is someone who will benefit from these cuts. Maybe it's someone who plans to invest in a private jail.

I remember this from 2010. I was knocking on doors helping a friend's political campaign. At one door, there was an older gentleman who said to me, "I don't have any kids going to school now. Why should any of my tax money go to the school system?"

Since I didn't want to turn him against my candidate, I nodded as if he had said something wise and insightful. My private reaction was the exact opposite. Sure, why pay taxes for education if your children aren't going to school anymore? How else could you benefit from schools?

I mean, it's not like an educated workforce makes more money, which can then get taxed and pay for your old age pension, and pave the roads, and get the snow cleared off your sidewalk. It's not like someone's child might get educated and come up with a business idea that will generate jobs, or that someone else's child might become a scientist and discover something that could help you ease your pains, cure a loved one's illness, or possibly even help you regain your hair (I'm still waiting on that one).

It's better to keep that money in your pocket. I'm sure it will go so much farther towards improving your lot in life.

Sarcasm aside, it concerns me that so many politicians (with help from the media) have conditioned people to become so short-sighted and self-centred. Maybe it's that a lot of people don't trust politicians to handle their tax money wisely. I understand because we see so many examples of tax money being wasted by various levels of government.

Giving governments less money won't stop them from wasting it. Keep an eye on the people you elect. Marking a ballot every so often is only the minimum. Get informed about what's going on. Demand value for your tax money. Write letters to your elected representatives. Get your neighbours to sign them, or write their own. A successful business is able to face the public and open the books to shareholders. Ask for explanations and don't accept sound bites in place of discussion.

At the same time, try to see the bigger picture. We're all in this together, so why not work together for the greater good?

◆

I think sometimes communities are not organizing around higher level issues. It's understandable because they need the immediate relief. If you're not secure in your personal life, or your family is not secure, it's difficult to get interested in issues that don't address your immediate needs and the immediate needs of the community.

When meaningful social change occurs, generally it's initiated by people in the privileged classes. They're the ones behind the charge because they have the time and the resources to push forward. You require people in those positions to facilitate change.

Here's an example. When women were legally recognized as persons in 1929, that was accomplished by the women known as The Famous Five. It was a reference case which was brought before the highest court in England. It was the efforts of these women that made it happen. They were well known even before they acted upon this.[1]

◆

It's the passive mentality of the people. I'd say this is more specific to Toronto, because I think Quebeckers have a different mentality than us. They're more politicized. You'll see things happen here and we'll keep quiet about them. For example, there was the G20 which had the biggest mass arrests in Canadian history, and we were relatively nonchalant about it. We even had the mayor, a well known progressive, pass a motion praising the police for a job well done.[2] If something like that happened in Quebec, you'd see some feedback.

◆

People will say that they don't have any input, and that's why they won't show up at election time. They'll say their vote doesn't make any difference, the politicians will do what they want anyway - it's the apathy.

The challenge that everybody throws at people, at the workplace, shopping, all those small "cheats" that they have to swallow, it keeps them busy. I call them "cheats" because these things cheat people of their time and their alertness.

Politics is in the background and elections every four years is when the folks who want to get elected show themselves. They're forgotten once the election is over. A lot of people don't even know who their representatives are. The three levels of government is another challenge.[3] And when there's a report on the radio, it passes too fast so people don't realize government is involved in the story, so people just let it pass away.

Unless you have some kind of education, you won't get the story no matter how important it is. When the politicians make decisions, they know we don't care. They know very well how much they can get away with, and the Senate scandal exposed a lot of it. Mike Duffy went a little bit too far, I guess.[4]

◆

It's probably not intentional (is my paranoia showing?), but when it comes to getting things done politically, the dice are somewhat stacked against Jane-Finch. Most of the day to day issues that people face belong to the municipal level of government. This includes subsidized housing, Ontario Works, transit, police, community centres, and parks. That's the responsibility of Toronto City Hall and your local councillor. There are a lot of people in Jane-Finch, so you'd think if we all got together, we could pressure our councillor and get things done.

That's not how things line up. The Jane-Finch area is divided between Wards 7, 8, and 9. If you live on either side of Jane Street north of Finch, you're in Ward 8 and so it stays south of Finch on the east side until you come to Grandravine. Then you're in Ward 9. The apartments and social housing that are south of Finch and on the west side of Jane? That's part of Ward 7.

What are the political implications? Suppose there's an issue at the housing complex on Dune Grassway or one of the apartment buildings on Firgrove Crescent (they are located next to each other). The problem is that if the Ward 7 councillor wants to look at issues that will garner the most votes, there are a lot of voters living in houses over in the Finch-Islington area. Though you wouldn't know it if you simply drove along Jane Street, there is a huge residential development inside that southwest corner of Jane and Finch, with even more located further south in the Jane-Sheppard area. That makes for a large group of voters that complement the ones in Finch-Islington.

If you live in the Grassways, your instinct might be to join forces with the people living in Yorkwoods Village across the street from you on Jane Street, but they don't live in your Ward. You'd have to try and connect with the apartments down at Jane and Chalkfarm, or the housing complex over at Ardwick Boulevard. Neither is particularly close, especially if you don't have a car.

It's the same deal with the southeast corner of Jane-Finch. TCH manages a great deal of housing in the area bounded by Jane, Finch, and Sheppard Avenue West, but Grandravine Drive divides it between Wards 8 and 9, going right through the centre of Yorkwoods Village.

I think it would be better if the Jane-Finch area had one councillor rather than three. Other Toronto neighbourhoods are basically located within one political boundary, such as Regent Park (Ward 28), Malvern (Ward 42), and Lawrence Heights (Ward 15).

I saw this happen in the past few municipal elections, where at least one would-be challenger looked at the population of Jane-Finch and thought building support in the area would help them upset the incumbent. Whether it was Ward 7 or Ward 8, the candidate thought this strategy would secure a strong showing, not realizing that a lot of the people just can't vote for you.

And it works the other way, too. As a candidate, you're only allowed to spend so much in an election campaign. Maybe in your heart, you really want to do something for Jane-Finch, but the cold numbers tell you that your campaign needs to go where the votes are. So the people of Jane-Finch (those that are in your Ward) don't see you, which means they won't vote for you. People are told they need to go out and vote, yet in a system like ours, there are so many ways that their vote doesn't really matter.

◆

A lot of people in Jane-Finch who work two or three jobs will be paying taxes. Yet a lot of them won't vote because they don't trust the government. Their tax dollars are there, so they do have a say. There is money, I don't mean funding, but money that comes through taxes. Look at wealthier areas and how they're doing. Maybe they have a stronger advocate, but why is it that those of us in poorer areas are losing?

◆

What's funny is that the zero tolerance approach started in the U.S., and now we're seeing various states trying to tell us that it didn't work for them, so we shouldn't take that approach. Their prisons are now overfilled. So they're moving away from it, yet the Harper government continues to embrace it.5 In the States, so many laws get passed, just like here with the omnibus laws, that people don't even know they're breaking the law and they don't know the consequences. That was the approach people like Stalin used, where you create so many laws that you can keep throwing laws at someone until you find one that sticks.

◆

They say they hold consultations with the people, but when they wanted to change the area's name to University Heights, nobody called me.6 They went to the retirement home and held the consultation there. The rest of the Jane-Finch community doesn't matter. They've got the spaces to hold consultations, we have the library, the community centres, so get the people together and talk to them. Have meetings in the community. Set up a social network so people will know what's going on.

◆

Since 9/11, CSIS and the RCMP have been looking at national security threats.7 Sources within those two have acknowledged that the external threat to Canada is quite low, certainly not as high as the U.S.A. or England.

Yet what's happened is that these two forces have been disproportionately funded by the government and what the government has done is engage in "threat amplification."

What this means is that they've created categories of terrorists and extremists that end up including environmental groups and community organizers. A lot of the people who were arrested prior to the G20 were community organizers. The new definition of a terrorist is someone who's against institutions and establishments.

The definition is so flexible that even members of a group like Jane-Finch On The Move could all be on a CSIS threat list and we wouldn't be aware of it. We'd have no recourse against it because, unfortunately, when you're labeled as a national security threat even your rights under the Charter can be limited. There are people who've been arrested or identified for organizing a bus trip to a rally.

What's scary is that it's CSIS and the RCMP who inform the local municipal police departments. So the word could come down to your local Division, the police will come looking for you, and you won't know why. And maybe the officers who bust you won't even know why themselves. They're all just following orders.

Notes

[1] The Famous Five were five prominent Alberta women: Emily Murphy (suffragist, reformer, writer, and first female magistrate in the British Empire), Nellie McClung (novelist, reformer, journalist, suffragist, elected to Alberta Legislature), Henrietta Muir Edwards (artist, legal expert, helped found the National Council of Women of Canada and the Victorian Order of Nurses), Louise McKinney (first woman elected as a Member of any Legislative Assembly in the British Empire), and Irene Parlby (first President of the United Farm Women's Association, elected to the Alberta Legislature, first female cabinet minister in Alberta). To learn more online, visit: http://www.famous5.ca/

[2] On July 7, 2010, Toronto City Council voted 36-0 to "commend the outstanding work" of Toronto Police Chief Bill Blair, his officers and other police forces working during the G20 summit in Toronto. Read the article here: http://preview.tinyurl.com/punxcq6

[3] There are three levels of government in Canada, each with its own set of responsibilities. This is explained further in the Appendix, under "Three Levels of Government."

[4] On November 5, 2013, Canadian Senators Mike Duffy, Patrick Brazeau and Pamela Wallin were stripped of all but their titles over charges of "gross negligence" in the use of their expense accounts. Read the article here: http://preview.tinyurl.com/ptbbtc5

[5] At the time of writing, Stephen Harper is Canada's Prime Minister.

[6] In October 2008, banners labeled "University Heights" were put up along Finch Avenue and Jane Street. This was part of a campaign to rebrand the area. The actual Jane-Finch intersection is divided by the city designated neighbourhoods of Black Creek (north of Finch) and Glenfield-Jane Heights (south of Finch). Toronto's Neighbourhood Profiles are here: http://preview.tinyurl.com/m3zxpz6

[7] CSIS and RCMP. According to their website, the role of CSIS (Canadian Security Intelligence Service) is "to investigate threats, analyze information and produce intelligence." Their programs are "are proactive and pre-emptive." The main priority is to counter terrorist violence, which is considered "a very real threat to our national security." You can learn more here: https://www.csis-scrs.gc.ca/bts/rlfcss-eng.asp

The Royal Canadian Mounted Police force was established in 1873 and provides police services across most of Canada excluding the provinces of Ontario and Quebec. According to their website, the RCMP's current scope of operations "includes organized crime, terrorism, illicit drugs, economic crimes and offences that threaten the integrity of Canada's national borders." You can learn more here: http://www.rcmp-grc.gc.ca/index-eng.htm

My Story - Eight (Female)

"The system has made our marriage a long distance relationship."

I met the man who would be my husband in June 2004 right at the intersection of Jane Street and Sheppard Avenue. I was on the way to visit my sister who lived in the area at the time. He approached me while I was waiting for the bus. I remember him being a complete gentleman which is the only reason he was able to get and keep my attention.

We were both twenty-three years old when we eloped at the North York Civic Centre, June 2005, on his birthday, in the presence of my sister and the father of her children. We kept it quiet for a while because our families thought it was too soon and we were too young.

My husband was going back and forth to court since 2001 dealing with some trouble he found himself in as a youth. When the trial was over, he was told to leave the country. I remember the staff at 6900 Airport Road saying, "Well, it's time to take a vacation."[1]

We thought so too, but some vacation it turned out to be, nearly nine years later. He departed two months earlier than the deadline, tired of fighting the system and eager to make things right. The fact that he had been here in Canada since the age of eleven and graduated from high school (Grade Thirteen with honors and receiving his Ontario Secondary School Diploma), didn't seem to make much of a difference. I guess when you're caught up in the system you are a number rather than an individual being.

I have made my relationship work, and it's been long-distance for a very long time. He's on the Islands and I'm here, so I have to travel back and forth to make things work until he's able to get back to Canada. We have both managed to make it work.

I will never forget this one time that I traveled in 2009. I was returning from Jamaica on an evening flight. We landed and I retrieved my belongings and continued to customs. I was told to go to the back for a secondary examination which turned into a nightmare.

I believe there was a rookie on shift that night looking to make his first big break because he mistakenly held me in detainment for suspicion of illegal narcotics in or on my body. I was held in custody and ill-treated for over eighteen hours by the Canada Border Services Agency (CBSA).

They wanted me to remove my clothing to be searched and when I refused, about three to four officers stripped off all my clothing down to nothing. They made me squat and shined flashlights into my private area. They also brought me to a cell and locked me in, slamming chairs against the door so I couldn't sleep.

I was really tired. The officers provoked me, told me I was lying about having nothing, presumed me guilty without a trial. I was even forced to have bowel movements and when I tried about three times, they said it wasn't enough. According to them, I couldn't leave until I produced a sufficient amount.

After much torture, I asked for the senior officer and told them I needed medical attention. I was rushed to the hospital through the airport, with many people watching. The doctor was able to give me an ultrasound as I was experiencing stomach pains after the strain. He reported back that I had nothing foreign in my abdomen.

When CBSA saw this they had no choice but to release me after escorting me out to the hospital and back to the airport in handcuffs. People were looking at me like I was a criminal. It was one of the worse days of my life. Up to this very day, I feel violated.

I've never been the same since then. Never received any justice besides a letter with somewhat of a lousy apology and a promise for a smooth path in future travels. My doctor keeps a close eye on me.

This makes my husband and I very nervous when it's time to travel. I thought about relocating to Jamaica but I am a full-time worker with benefits. I have plans to return to school to pursue International Business Administration and we are expecting our first child. This distance is hindering our progress because we don't know what to expect.

For the last seven years or so, we want to be together so much in our relationship, but instead there's this big obstacle making it so difficult for us. Every time we take two steps forward, here comes another obstacle and we have to take ten steps back. There's always this wedge. We all make mistakes and have to pay for them, but in this case I'm sure it's been over ten years since it's been paid for.

Every time you think you're progressing, the bureaucrats throw something else at you. "You have to do this," or "we need this," or "the law's changed," or "the fees have gone up."

I have been trying to get my husband here for so long now. In a way, it's almost like a "forbidden love," and it certainly has the potential to become something very powerful. My husband left in 2006, and since

2007 we have been working on reuniting. We have to go through the paperwork, his pardons, and need more money for his fees. All the traveling to and from Jamaica is getting quite expensive as well. We could be using those funds to buy real estate.

It's only a matter of time. We chose not to use a lawyer and face this on our own. I think when the bureaucrats see that we're not using a lawyer, they make it a little harder. Lawyers talk the language and know what to do to get ahead. Here we are, two individuals who think we can work against that and they push us back. But we're determined. And we're very close. When we do get there, we'll be very appreciative of what we have because we know what it's like to not have it.

Lawyers can play with you because they know you're vulnerable and I have watched a lot of people go through that as well. We originally thought about getting a lawyer, and I watched friends and people I know get abused by their lawyer and nothing really came out of it. I have a friend who paid a lawyer $1500 and she did not even get her application sent in because she couldn't contact the lawyer again. It's those kind of things that made my spouse and I very nervous and decide to take the plunge and do it ourselves.

Now I'm seeing how the immigration system and the justice system will work with you if you don't have those resources and you're not using a lawyer and paying so many thousands of dollars. If you're a little fish in a big tank of sharks, they just don't have time to deal with you and they keep pushing you back unless you're very determined. It takes longer to get where you need to go when you don't spend the money. It's all about money, I guess. And maybe there's also a question of who you know.

Our struggle has been a long one. My husband was eighteen when he got into the trouble that got him sent back, and now when he's trying to live a productive life, those little things come back to haunt him.

Although he wants to make things right, they want to keep him in the system, they want to keep a tab on him, they want to know what's going on - they don't want to let him go. It's hard for him to get out of that. It's the Canadian government that is creating the problems. I was born here, but he was not. But what about my basic human rights? What about my right to love and be loved - does that have to come with a large price tag?

Notes

[1] There is a Canada Border Services Agency (CBSA) office located at 6900 Airport Road, Mississauga.

Money, Motivation, Media, and More

Members sound off on topics that didn't fit under other headings.

You don't want to complain, because then you get penalized. That's why you don't say anything about anything, because then it gets taken away. If I complain about part of a program, those who fund it take away the entire program.

◆

Everyone has a purpose here on earth. Anything that you're good at, that is your purpose here. I see that my purpose here is looking after my family. If I were to come back in this world, I wouldn't do it again (look after my family) because it was hard work. If I was living in the States, I would have liked to try acting. It would be difficult to get acting jobs being a black person. If I'm doing something and I don't see any results, I will quit.

◆

Poverty is here in Jane-Finch, but you don't see it. You go downtown, you see the people on the street with their faces bleeding and broken.

◆

This area has a lot of heart. You go to other communities and you don't find this spirit that they have here. It's just that they lack some of the things they need.

◆

This is a big problem for the youth. If you want to get an education and you don't get a grant, you've got a huge debt. It's such a big struggle that it's hard not to just give up.

◆

What's this talk about grants? I don't see the grants. People are saying there are grants here and there. We don't know how to apply for grants.

The people who have the money don't know how to promote the existence of these grants properly. They don't let you know what's going on in the community. They get the money, and then they say the youth don't come out. The youth aren't coming out because nobody knows about it. They should knock on doors and talk to the youths, tell them about the programs. During the school year, go to the schools around three to four (p.m.), because that's where the youth will be.

The youth aren't allowed to get grants. It's only the agencies and organizations who get the grants. That's because they don't trust the youth with money, and they don't trust the people in this community with money.

◆

So I hear part of the issue with programs and grants is the lack of promotion. I can attest that organizations hand out flyers all the time. So what is happening when people get the flyers? The flyers contain information. A lot of times you knock on doors and no one answers. How do you co-ordinate the time when you can find the individual?

◆

What I hear is that people living in Jane and Finch can become complacent, and that the motivation is not there. If people want to do something, but can't get the help and support, they get down, they lose that motivation and give up.

◆

In my opinion, the real estate people are the ones that push the bad image in order to benefit from real estate sales. One side will say, "Oh yeah, this is a bad neighbourhood, you have to sell to get out of here." Then when new people come in, they would come up with the benefits of the neighbourhood. So it was a motivation for them to push this image which is definitely not true because when you look at the rest of the city, other places have the same trouble that they claim we have here.

◆

When you're looking at families in poor neighbourhoods, you need to look holistically at the area. The kind of help given is restrictive. Look at the Food Bank - now you can't choose what you want, they give you prepackaged bags. Of course, people used to fight over the food back then. But now people don't use everything because it's not what they like. A lot of the cans are dented. People don't want dented cans because the inside of the cans are coated with chemicals. If the coating is broken, the chemicals get into the food. So people will throw out dented cans. The Food Bank gives you what they have.

◆

This emphasis on image is killing us all. The kids all want to look like the people on TV. This costs a lot of money. They want the high end clothes, the hair extensions, and they don't have the money, so they keep stealing to feed this habit. I care about food, so my house is full of food. Someone comes by and asks why there's so much food in my house, when there's no food in theirs. But you've got a car, and you've got nice clothes.

◆

You have all these little things, all these little obstacles. For example, there are programs to watch your kids until six p.m. But you have to pick up your kid after school and take him to the program. You have to sacrifice one or the other.

◆

My issue with Jane-Finch is that people are not motivated to leave Jane-Finch. They all want to stay here, live paycheck to paycheck, just because they're so used to it. They say, "This is all I know." If you're not trying to explore, what will you know?

◆

I came here in 1970 - I was a kid then. I started working when I was fifteen, working Friday nights and all day Saturday at the Granite Club. When I started, I got three dollars an hour because I had no experience. They had three pay grids. The people with experience got more.

I've always worked in the food service industry because you could make good money in tips. You'd make more in tips than in wages. Bank tellers were making $2.75 an hour back then - can you believe that?

Where else did I work? There were so many places after the Granite Club. I worked at two Fran's locations on Yonge Street, first the one at Eglinton Avenue, then the location at St. Clair Avenue West. There was a restaurant at the Eaton Centre, and that place had good tips.

I saw an advertisement for the Wendy's (fast food restaurant) at Yonge and Charles Street. I started off there fixing the food and giving it to the customer. Back then, Wendy's used to have a salad bar and I was in charge of keeping that, too. I won first prize for how I took care of the salad bar. Because of how well I worked, they moved me up to cash, then made me a co-leader, which paid more. I could get there in the morning before the manager and open the store. At night, I could close. I could tell the workers what to do.

The manager was very nice and asked if I wanted to learn to be a manager. So he trained me. Every day I'd watch how things were done. There was a lot to know, even all the ingredients. We made the hamburgers in the store. I got to do the written test and I passed. Later, I went to run the Wendy's at Dundas and Yonge.

Speaking of Wendy's, I used to make the chili. A lot of the ingredients came from the U.S., so we just had to add tomatoes, green onions, and peppers. When I make chili at home, I put in celery instead. The other workers cried when they had to peel and chop onions, but it didn't bother me.

While I was working at Wendy's, I was studying to become a dietitian. When I passed, I quit Wendy's and went to work at Women's

College Hospital. I got sick about four years ago, and had to go on two year's sick leave. If I want to go back and work there full-time, I could. Right now, I'm not able to take on a full-time schedule. I still drop by if they need someone to fill in.

If I could change one thing about Jane-Finch, it would be that when you fill out a job application, you don't have to leave out that you live in Jane-Finch.

◆

I've been watching. At the end of the month when the Baby Bonus runs out, there aren't any sales on food. Also at the middle of the month, when the Baby Bonus comes in, there are no sales. We have to maximize our money, so we look at the reduced produce. I'm pinching and balancing. If I go to McDonald's or KFC, I have to sacrifice groceries. If I buy nice clothes, I can't buy food. I don't go shopping and waste my money. Sometimes I wish I could drink a beer or something.

◆

I was watching Dr. Oz and he was saying how we can use coconut flour, almond flour, and so on to help us improve our health. I go into a speciality store to buy this food, and I walk right out. These foods are too expensive. The welfare won't give us enough money, so I'm buying reduced food. These reduced vegetables rot quickly.

◆

This is another part of the problem. So many of the people have illnesses or chronic pains but they can't afford to do anything about it. Acupuncture might work for my pains, but I can't afford that.

Back in Jamaica, we used leaves and herbs for things like colds and measles. Here we need to take all these commercial pills that have so many side effects. Years of taking aspirin for my pains gave me ulcers. If you use the old remedies instead of pills that don't really work, you get accused of not taking proper care of your children.

◆

How does a poor person who has no resources survive here? Back in Jamaica, there are all kinds of produce growing, so it's different there. You go out in the country, and there's bananas, pears, akees, yams. And no one gets sick.

We have to balance the past with the present so that we can survive. The government gives us money and they see it as giving us luxuries.

When the Public Health came to my house, they'd tell me what I could and couldn't feed my babies. I'd agree, but when they left, I'd go back to what worked for me. They aren't putting money into my pocket, buying my food, paying my rent.

◆

One thing that I found very respectful is how one of my neighbours deals with language differences. She's from Africa, and English is not anyone's first language in her house. When a visitor goes into that house, it immediately becomes an English-speaking area. This is the first person that I ever met who takes that very seriously. Even if they're struggling with some of the words, they'll turn to me to help them figure it out rather than speak in a language which I (or any other visitor) would not understand. "Right now, we're equal," she'll say. There's nothing hidden and she doesn't want anyone to feel uncomfortable. Even if it's something like telling her children to eat their food, visitors should know what's being said. That's how she looks at being in Canada.

◆

More prisons only build more criminals - it's not a solution. I worked in the Jamaican penal system. There's a problem with people committing crimes while on probation - why not invest in electronic monitors like in the U.S.? I know the cost of these devices is an issue, but it pays off in the long run.

◆

If you ask me, the key is putting money into people's pockets. And by that, I mean the money goes straight into residents' pockets. Not into community services or programs or the people who run the programs, but into people's hands so they can buy things and save for their future.

I'm not against money being spent by various levels of government, I just don't believe it's the only model. From a commercial standpoint, our local shopping centres are drab and reflect an area where there isn't a lot of discretionary income.

What needs to happen is that we have to find ways to attract outside consumers to come to the area and spend money here. If we're being honest, the area is not completely low income. Many of the residential neighbourhoods are quite nice. Look at the cars parked in the driveways. It's just that these folks can drive to the nicer malls and shops located outside the area. The Yorkdale Mall is less then fifteen minutes away by car. When the subway is finished, people will find it even easier to travel to places like Yorkdale, the Eaton Centre, and even the Wal-Mart up on Jane and Highway Seven.

I propose that we use the arts as a way to draw in the money. For example, why not use murals? There is a wonderful mural on the side of 4400 Jane Street. The problem is that it's not visible from the street. As well, many of the local electrical boxes have been painted. They look great, but they're small and mostly located on side streets.

I say we go in your face and get audacious with murals. Both the Jane-Finch Mall and Yorkgate Mall have large stretches of blank wall facing out towards Jane Street and Finch Avenue. Why not cover these walls with huge murals, designed by local artists and painted by the artists and local youth? I know it's private property, but I would think if done properly, these murals would enhance the properties and attract outside attention and more customers. If the designs are created and chosen by local residents, there's less chance of vandalism. The mural at 4400 Jane Street has been untouched since its creation.

The media likes to describe Jane-Finch as a concrete corridor, so it's obvious they haven't really taken a look around. If they did, they'd notice most of those apartment buildings are surrounded by large tracts of land. For the most part, these chunks of land are nothing but wide expanses of mowed grass that no one ever walks upon. Nothing says "suburbs" like acres of mowed lawns.

These open spaces aren't really open, because they're either privately owned or TCH properties. However, why not look into putting up some low cost low maintenance plants and vegetation that would break up the green monotony and spruce up the area? What if large sections of Jane-Finch were to bloom every spring?

The goal is to make the Jane-Finch area something that will draw interest from across the city and beyond. Going back to the art theme, why not set up permanent art displays in both malls? Perhaps area students could compete in annual art contests, with the winning pieces put on display for an entire year. Displaying art by local talent can only build a stronger sense of community spirit.

It's all about giving people reasons to come to the area and stick around for a few hours. Keep them around long enough to spend money at local businesses. Get some of that traffic from the new subway stations coming our way.[1] If the concern is that people will stay away because of the area's bad reputation, let's recall that other Toronto neighbourhoods have overcome stigma.

Perception is reality. If Jane-Finch looks bleak and barren (or if we keep talking like the area is bleak and barren), that will keep people away. People don't need to want to live here, as we have plenty of residents who appreciate what we have. People only need to want to come visit for a bit, enjoy themselves and hopefully come back another time.

◆

An issue with Jane-Finch is that people don't have. Everything's a donation. And people want credit for what they give: "it's a donation." How are we supposed to have pride? If you join a program, people are going to say, "Oh those people (taking the program) need it. They can't afford it." So you feel ashamed to put your kids in the programs, because everyone has to know it's a charity: "This person donated it, that person donated it, poor Jane and Finch!"

What we don't need are temporary fixes. This is what gets donated. We need stuff that is more long term.

◆

Why would people leave Jane-Finch? They feel it's an area where the problems aren't going to go away, the problems will always be here. The media will always put it down, the resources will always be lacking, instead of trying to reinvent or reinvest, and looking for ways to give back and empower the people who are here. That way, it's not a place that you're trying to get out of, it's a place where you feel comfortable living.

Sometimes I feel that it is a place where you feel so defeated that maybe you do want to get away.

You have these charts that list poverty by postal code and you see your area listed. You begin to think, "What am I doing here? What future do I have in a place like this?"

And you look around and they want to close your hospital, they want to close your schools, and you think, "How can I fight this? How can I fight a system that is already doing this? I might as well go somewhere where there are more of the resources needed."

◆

A lot of things go unsolved in this community. Nobody knows anything. Nobody sees anything. Nobody wants to put themselves on the line. Sure, there's a lot of heart in Jane-Finch, but people are very much into themselves.

I had a friend whose uncle came down from the north somewhere. He came to visit in Jane-Finch and said that nobody smiles. Everybody is so serious, nobody says good morning, good afternoon, like they would where he comes from. You only find that friendliness in the older people. There's a lack of trust, no one wants to say anything.

Is that coldness specific to Jane-Finch and other inner cities? I don't find other parts of Toronto to be much more inviting. In fact, I've heard from visitors that Toronto is a cold city. I recall going to American cities and being surprised that people would talk to me without any reason.

I was talking to a lady the other day and she said, "This place is not like back home, which was like a village. Everybody was helping everybody with the kids, and looking out for each other. You come here and you don't have anybody. You're alone. If you don't have a day care to watch your kids, you're finished."

If you don't have a day care and your children are running around, you're a bad parent. If they take your kids and watch them for you, they sit around and talk about how you're a bad parent, how you let your kids outside or how you're never there.

People would rather judge you than stretch out that hand to help. It's not like back home where you don't have to worry about certain things. Go to the store and leave your child in the park, come back and you know that your neighbour or someone from the community is watching your house. Here it's a little more bleak, you can't that do here.

◆

You don't have to be one who submits to a boss. If you have enough drive, common sense, and knowledge, you could probably operate your own business. People aren't told that often enough. If you have a skill, capitalize on it. Try to do something so that you're not dependent on two or three minimum wage jobs for your survival. There are ways out. Others have found a way. They had knowledge of something that they could use. Not of all them had advanced degrees from school. Some of them started with small businesses that became something else.

◆

There was a time when a person could make a good living from manual labour. No real skills were required, other than those gathered while on the job, maybe learning how to run machinery or something. Generations of immigrants thrived because of this. Now we're seeing a lot of downward pressure being applied to wages. Give it time and it won't be just "unskilled" positions that feel the squeeze.

If I headed up a corporation, maybe I'd want my workers to work for ten dollars an hour and be grateful for it. Maybe the system is designed to break people down so there's a supply of cheap labour. People will flip your burgers because they've got nowhere better to go.

◆

People get comfortable making a certain amount of money because if they go beyond that, they have to fear their rent being raised (geared to income). So they keep their income in a certain bracket to avoid an increase or even paying market rent, because they can't afford it. That's why they're living in government housing, because they're working those two or three jobs and not even making one salary. So they're living in that fear, and some are even living on government assistance

◆

Where is the money going? Personally, I've passed through a few of the youth programs that should be doing more for the residents but there's something lacking. This pool of money is there for certain things, yet you look at the circumstances, the programming, the activities that are taking place, and it's not matching up. I think that's another area that needs more accountability.

Everything's being spread too thin. Everyone's so busy working individually on their own project or interest. If we were organized together, working on one area or one specific thing at a time, we could see where the funding went, and then we move on to the next one. We need more partnerships and that's with bigger organizations and grassroots groups. Because you need grassroots - they are the ones on the ground, the ones working with the residents.

You can be an agency overlooking everything but until you come down to the grassroots, communicating and partnering with these residents, it's rather pointless because you're making assumptions - you're not directly working with these people. If you're going to employ people, it should be residents that get employed. People will come in with degrees and tell people what to do, but they won't or can't give practical ideas on how to get things done.

◆

I suppose people will always find things to get angry over. I just wish they could widen their aim. For example, you get talking with people about things that make them angry and for a lot of them, the topic of welfare comes up really fast. They get so angry about how their tax dollars go to people on welfare. Their hard earned money is going to people who don't work and just sit around all day.

Okay, let's not argue about the rights and wrongs of welfare. Let's admit some people abuse welfare, so long as we also admit that some people really need it. That being said, one thing about people on welfare is that they spend their welfare cheque. It's not like they're so well off that they cash the cheque and bank it. No, that money goes for food, goes for clothing, and yes, maybe it goes to buy the kids a video game.

The point is that the money is being spent. How is that not helping the economy? The money goes into the pockets of store owners, services, etc., which means it gets taxed sooner or later. At least the money is in play, and it's like planting seeds - you never know what might sprout.

Compare that to all these companies getting tax cuts. Ontario's got one of the lowest corporate tax rates anywhere, yet businesses keep calling for more tax cuts.[2]

We're told it's good for business, because companies will take that money and invest it, growing their businesses, and I guess making life better for all of us eventually. Only if you read the newspapers, you read that a lot of these companies are just socking away this money. Last time I looked, tax cuts are also funded by taxpayer money. All that money is sitting around, and still we keep giving companies more. How come people don't get mad at that? Well, some do, but they tend to be the same people who don't complain about folks on welfare. Can you imagine how people would react if we found out welfare recipients were getting so much money they were able to sock away a good chunk each month?

I get the feeling that a lot of people are somehow taught that there are things and people they can get angry about, such as folks on welfare, but don't even think of rocking the boat and complaining about people who make money. Even if they're making that money off you. When someone is driving a fancy car that is leased, that's usually written off as a business expense. Who do you think pays for that? It's the same taxpayer who's paying for a single mother's welfare. If you want to get mad at a young mother feeding her kid with "your" money, go ahead. It's your blood pressure. But why aren't you equally mad at the guy tooling around in a Porsche which is also paid with "your" money?

◆

A lot of these guys don't know money. They think it's hard to come by, but it's not if you have the actual skills and mind set. It's just paper at the end of the day. It's a frame of mind, it's how you look at it and I guess being in communities where you are already so dependent on resources from the government, you don't see money as something that is easy to come by, you see it as something that is challenging and difficult to obtain. It's a fear that you can't do it, that you can't be more than just that.

It's about creating an awareness. There are successful people who came from Jane-Finch who can be models. They can come back and say how they did it. Because it's hard to see it when you're sitting in a rundown school and a rundown house. Let's take them out of that environment and show them that there are other things they can aim for. There might be something that lets them see a different perspective, "I've learned this by seeing it."

◆

A few years ago, I decided to Google "Jane-Finch" and see what information was available from a historical standpoint. I was more than a bit surprised to find articles that said residents were complaining about conditions in the area since at least the early 1970s.

That's a long time to be complaining. That's a long time waiting for things to get better.

It's not like Jane-Finch is being ignored. There are a lot of organizations and groups in the area which offer programs and services. And I have heard that a lot of government money is poured into Jane-Finch, but I can't find an actual dollar amount to back this up. I do know the City of Toronto made more money available for various initiatives after Jane-Finch was designated a "Priority Area" in 2005.

This would be a good thing, right?

I wonder. It was four or five summers ago that a friend invited me to show up at a local school. Area residents were invited to be interviewed. There was quite the turn out, possibly sparked by the offer of free lunches (which were tasty). I was basically a fly on the wall, walking by groups of people and listening in. If I had any greater purpose for being there, I don't remember it now.

I do remember this. One woman said, "I've lived here for thirty years. We keep getting asked about the problems here, but no one ever does anything about it."

Well, that's not entirely true. There are a lot of local groups and organizations in the area. That's doing something, isn't it?

Let's make it clear that I'm not criticizing the work of these organizations. A lot of good work is done by dedicated people. Instead, I'm questioning the overall set up.

If a community is in need of various services, why do we look to organizations to provide them? Where's the government in all this? Organizations need funds to operate. Where do the funds come from? From what I know, the money either comes from large charitable organizations or the money comes from some level of government, be it municipal, provincial, or federal. Often, it's a combination of the two.

So in the end, the money is mostly coming from our pockets. It's either from taxes, or from donating to a charity. Even if you don't donate directly, charities get tax breaks, which come from the pockets of taxpayers, so you're still paying for it.

Wouldn't it be more efficient if the government provided these services directly? Are services somehow better provided when the money has to go through some charity with its own level of management before it gets to a local organization? I got confused just saying that sentence, so I'm guessing the answer will lean towards the negative.

Most of these local organizations have to devote time and effort to get funding. Charities dedicate a lot of their time and effort to get donations. As for governments, they have this rather effective tool set up to raise funds called taxes. I am free to ignore letters that ask me to contribute to a charitable cause, but I can't ignore the taxman.

My point is that we give money to various levels of government, and at every election, we choose people to represent us at these various levels. So, if certain areas have particular concerns or problems, why do we expect individuals or small groups to come up with solutions? In that respect, Jane-Finch is lucky that people have come together to create organizations to bridge the gaps.

However, I can't help but think these are basically band-aid solutions which let our governments off the hook. What happens if your area doesn't have people who can organize, or know how to tap funders? And I said Jane-Finch was "lucky," but people here have been complaining for over forty years now. How lucky is that?

If you really want to deal with social issues, you need to look at the fundamentals of your society and lay the groundwork for some real change. That's the kind of vision you'd want from a government. Instead, we get band-aid solutions, handed out when times are good and there's votes to be had, and cut back when times are tight and there's different votes to be wooed.

◆

I started taking programs when my first son was little. I wasn't treated too well by the workers. I was treated like I was stupid. I was new to the country, couldn't speak English too well, so I stopped after a few classes. A few years later, I applied for child care when I was going to 4401 Driftwood Avenue (Driftwood Community Centre) to learn English.

My husband could speak English and French. He'd visit his sister and speak French. I was sure they were talking about me. My husband didn't want me to learn English, so I went to his parents to make them change his mind. This was before I got pregnant. I learned the basics. I saw Egyptian people there. We went to gossip - I was young back then! We had coffee and talked.

◆

I come here (Driftwood Community Centre) every week for a cooking class. We cook vegetarian food, then we sit and eat as a group. I've been taking programs for twenty-five to thirty years. When I had my son, I was very depressed. So they sent me to YWCA, and from there I ended at Driftwood Community Centre for a program.

I was lucky because the woman who was running the depression class was very good. What I learned from her made me better. I went for two years then took a one year break, then another two years. Someone working in Jane/Finch Community and Family Centre would stay in touch with me.

◆

I guess you pretty much accept failure for what it is. We're living in what they once called middle class, but it's more like poor class. There really isn't any middle class as things are getting rough.

As a way of being more independent and not reliant on government support, it would be a positive move for those of us who are community organizers and grassroots groups to organize around teaching our residents how to be more financially independent. Perhaps they could be their own employers.

There's a lack of jobs here and all over the world. There's always a cap on what you can make if you work for someone else. I believe people have natural skills that they probably don't know how to capitalize upon. Or maybe they came from another country where they had skills. Maybe they were a nurse, or a chef, but then they come here and have to start again from scratch.

If you have the natural skills, there are ways you can go around and be your own employer in a way that you could capitalize on the skills you already have. It would be good to organize around this. Of course we would need funding for this, but it's what a lot of our organizations should be doing. It can get very discouraging to try and get change happening.

◆

When it comes to taking advantage of opportunities, or creating opportunities where there may not seem to be any, I think we forget that we still have the freedom to refuse to take no for an answer.

It does seem that there are a lot of barriers set up in our community, particularly when it comes to opportunities. So we'll hear that there's no money, no resources, no political will, and so on, yet there's no law that says we have to take this to heart and give up.

For instance, if you're getting a lousy education, we still have a good library system. Read how others have succeeded, learn from the trials and tribulations of others, fill your head with knowledge and inspiration. True, it may be a hard road to travel. Many have had a easier route, but no matter how tough it is for you, there is always someone who had it tougher. And they made it. So why not you?

◆

I work retail in a big mall. I would like to be in charge of my own business, my own brand. I haven't received the help to achieve what I want. It's so frustrating, because no one wants to help you. I don't know what they want. I try, and try and try.

I'm twenty-one: the dream is in my head but it's so far to reach. And it hurts, and it makes you want to give up. But what can I do? You have to work for someone. When you try to work for yourself, it's just not possible, it's so hard. My hopes are to get out of Jane-Finch, to be a successful individual, to have my own business, to be in charge, to help others that started where I started from and uplift them.

Part of the problem that I get from others is that a lot of blacks don't like to help our own. There's not the support. No one wants to be a mentor. No one wants to say, "This is what you want. I have gone through it, and I am willing to help you to get out."

The people I've spoken to who've done well and were able to leave Jane and Finch, they're not coming back. They should come in, do workshops, talk and let us see how they did it. Then it's up to the individual themselves to follow up and carry it out.

I need someone to talk me through, to tell me what I need to get. I go around to the resources here and it hasn't gotten me anywhere. I'm still in the same place. The resources here - you can only stay for six months and then they close your case and they move on to the next person. They're not really helping you. They say they're helping you and calling you every two months to see how things are going, but that's not really help. They'll call you when there's a job fair happening or if they hear anything, but that's about it. They aren't doing the interesting work that they should be doing or anything that takes that extra step in helping someone. They just do what their job requires them to do.

Instead, they need to be passionate about what they're going to do. See it through to the end.

If my dreams don't come true, I'll be so hurt. I don't know what will happen to me. I don't feel like this is my reality. Everyday, I just feel like I'm not supposed to be here. I gave myself ten years. I've got nine more to go. And if I'm not where I want to be, I'm going to stop denying reality and accept where I am.

Notes

1 The Toronto-York Spadina Subway Extension will include the Finch West station, located at the intersection of Keele Street and Finch Avenue West. This is two kilometres away from the Jane-Finch intersection. The new station is currently scheduled to open in fall 2016. There will also be a subway station on Steeles Avenue West (Pioneer Village). This will be three kilometres away from the Jane-Finch intersection, but likely more convenient for residents living north of the intersection. For example, it will be within walking distance for those living in the Driftwood-Shoreham area.

2 "The combined federal-Ontario rate was slashed from 45 per cent in 1999 to 30 per cent in 2010." "The federal corporate tax rate is falling to 15 per cent next year. If Ontario restored a 14-per-cent provincial rate, the combined rate would be 29 per cent ... American state governments also levy corporate taxes, producing combined rates around 40 per cent in the Great Lakes states. A 29-percent combined rate would keep Ontario at the low end of the world's other major economies: Japan (40 per cent), Brazil (34 per cent), India (34 per cent), France (33 per cent), Italy (31 per cent), Germany (29 per cent), the United Kingdom (26 per cent) and China (25 per cent)." Erin Weir, "Corporate Taxes are Low Enough," *Ottawa Citizen*, September 27, 2011

Appendix

Defining Jane-Finch

For all the talk about a Jane-Finch community, there isn't a clear definition of this community's boundaries. In fact, "Jane-Finch" has never been an official name for the area. It has been suggested that this came from a 1965 Toronto Daily Star story about a mother of eight forced to move to a townhouse in Jane and Finch.[1] Once in print, the phrase soon became a popular description of the general area.

An area name which has not proven popular is "Elia." This neighbourhood has the following boundaries: Highway 400 to the west, Steeles Avenue West north going east to Black Creek, south down the Creek turning east at the hydro corridor over to Keele Street (completely bypassing York University), and south to Sheppard Avenue West.[2]

Elia certainly sounds like the inspiration for a few of the suggested boundaries. One of the more common has Highway 400 as the western edge, Steeles Avenue West to the north, Sheppard Avenue West to the south, and Black Creek to the east.

York University offers a "wide" definition that has Jane-Finch neatly defined by four major roadways - Steeles to the north, Keele to the east, Highway 400 to the west, and Sheppard to the south.[3]

Wikipedia suggests Jane-Finch occupies a far more narrow area, one "bounded by Highway 400 to the west, Driftwood Avenue to the east, Grandravine Drive to the south, and Shoreham Drive to the north."[4]

And then there is the definition of Jane-Finch as a City of Toronto Priority Area. As always, Steeles Avenue West is the north boundary, ending east at Black Creek, but stretching west all the way to the Humber River (about five kilometres) which is the west boundary all the way south to Sheppard Avenue over to Jane Street and south to where Black Creek curves east.[5] This super sized Jane-Finch is an amalgamation of four separate city-defined neighbourhoods: Black Creek, Glenfield-Jane Heights, Humber Summit, and Humbermede.[6]

The symbolic drawback to the Priority definition is that the Jane-Finch intersection lies close to the eastern edge of the area. If there is ever going to be an official boundary for Jane-Finch, it should be centered around its namesake intersection.

Developing Jane-Finch

More often than not, an article about Jane-Finch will make reference to the rapid growth of the area. It's hard to overlook. According to at least one account, "from 1961 to 1971, the population increased an astronomical 2,438 per cent."[7]

I've been living in the Jane-Finch area ever since I was three, and grew up during the peak growth period. I have some memories of the area's development.

The most vivid one goes back to when I was seven years old, and coming home from school on the TTC. Looking back from a 2014 viewpoint, I'm amazed that there was a time period where no one questioned a seven year old riding public transit alone on a daily basis.

For some reason, the bus passed right by my normal stop, and I ended up in a construction site. It was winter, and I stepped into a mud patch. At least it looked like mud, but construction site mud must be part quicksand, because it grabbed my boot and wouldn't let go. The mud kept my boot as I limped home with one foot clad only in a sock. No one remembers if I ever got the boot back.

I was finally able to visualize the rapid growth when I went to the City Of Toronto Archives and found their collection of aerial photographs. Luckily, these photographs were taken almost every year from 1947 to 1992.[8] I was particularly interested in the unbroken run of photographs taken from 1959 to 1971.

Using Highway 400 as a marker, I was able to identify many of the changes in the area over the years. The process was not precise; I'd simply note the first year a particular building was clearly visible, unless that building was a school, in which case I got the date from the school's web site or from the nice people at the TDSB Museum and Archives.

If we consider "Jane-Finch" to encompass an area that is bounded in the east by Black Creek, to the south by Sheppard Avenue West, to the north by Steeles Avenue West, and to west by Highway 400, then the actual Jane-Finch intersection is roughly located in the centre.

Ironically, the intersection of Jane Street and Finch Avenue West was the last to be fully developed. In 1950, there was a farmhouse in the northeast corner of Jane and Finch. The other three corners were fields.

There is a photograph, taken in 1962, which shows cows grazing in a field on the southwest corner.

In 1963, construction crews began working in the southeast and northwest corners of Jane and Finch. By 1967, there was a gas station in the northwest corner. The Jane-Finch Mall would dominate the southeast corner by 1968. And the southwest corner? In 1968 it was still an empty field all the way west to the recently built York Finch Hospital and Westview Centennial Collegiate. The field stretched south all the way to Eddystone Road. Odds are good that the cows were gone.

The corner farm house was still standing in 1970. The southwest corner was still a field, but development was moving in. The writing was on the wall for that farm.

By 1971, the farm and related buildings were gone to make way for what would become the Palisades. In 1976, the first of the three buildings that line San Romanoway was built. And the southwest corner was developed when the Norfinch Shopping Centre opened in 1975.

As for that gas station sitting by itself in the northwest corner? It remained the sole occupant until 1991 when the Yorkgate Mall took over most of the block.

While it took a while for the centre to get developed, the surrounding area filled in much faster. One wonders what the inhabitants of that farm house thought as they saw all the construction vehicles driving along during the 1960s. One wonders where the cows ended up.

There is a perception that Jane-Finch is a concrete canyon. Go along Jane in either direction from Finch and it's pretty much apartment buildings, plazas, and townhouses (many of which are public housing). Turn off into any of the side streets and you enter 1960s suburbia.

That's how the area developed. In 1961, the Jane-Finch intersection was a rural centre. Yet the suburbs were already on the move. In the northwest corner of Jane and Sheppard Avenue West, the established homes along Sheppard and Stanley Road saw the start of a new subdivision branching off Laura Road in 1959.

By 1961, the houses on Stanley Road had been razed to make way for new housing and Stanley Public School. A year later, the entire development going north up to Frith Road was complete. In 1966, the Wycliffe Jane Plaza opened at the corner of Jane and Sheppard.

On the other side of that corner, work began on the development anchored around Spenvalley Drive in 1960. In 1962, No. 31 Police Station opened on 1906 Sheppard Avenue West. By 1965, construction was complete until the Northwoods Golf Course was sold and turned into additional housing in 1980. This includes the Ontario Housing

Corporation (OHC) units built along the north side of Sheppard Avenue West (Sheppard Yatescastle).

Local schooling was provided in 1964 by St. Jane Frances Catholic School which opened at 2745 Jane Street, and Spenvalley Public School which was built just up the road at 108 Spenvalley Drive. Historical note: in 1983, the building which housed Spenvalley was leased from the Board of Education to become Blessed Margherita of Citta di Castello Catholic School.

Oakdale Junior High (later Middle School) was opened in 1965 at 315 Grandravine Drive. By 1967, St. Jane Frances was expanded, and the Jane-Sheppard Mall opened across the street at 2669 Jane Street.

Directly across the street from the Finch farmhouse, the southeast corner was cleared by 1963. By 1965, houses were built all along the northern half of Driftwood down to Yorkwoods Gate, including Venetian Crescent, Topcliff Avenue, Yellowstone Street, and Demaris Avenue. OHC units were built at 20 Yellowstone (Finch Topcliffe). Topcliff Public School opened at 65 Topcliff Avenue that year.

In 1966, the Yorkwoods Plaza was built at 2845 Jane Street on the north side of Yorkwoods Gate. And in 1967, the tide of construction swept over to the other side of Yorkwoods Gate. Yorkwoods Public School opened at 25 Yorkwoods Gate. OHC units that would be part of Yorkwoods Village were built at 10-44 Driftwood Avenue and would extend over to Grandravine Drive the next year.

The pitter patter of bulldozers and dump trucks didn't shake the foundations of our farmhouse until 1964. Driftwood Avenue was opened up to Niska Road, and the subdivision rapidly filled up with houses. Driftwood Public School was built in 1965. Two years later, the townhouses between Finch and Potsdam Road were built.

The fastest development may have been in the northwest section. This would be the area bounded by Highway 400 to the west, Finch to the south, Jane to the east, and north to Steeles. Other than a few buildings just off Jane Street, the area was field until 1962. That was when work begun on what would be Norfinch Drive, running parallel to the highway.

Within a few years, houses popped up along the subdivision bracketed by Hullmar Drive and Gosford Boulevard going north to Shoreham Drive, and a bit closer to Steeles Avenue West. Gosford Public School was built at 30 Gosford Boulevard in 1963, and Blacksmith Public School opened in 1967 at 45 Blacksmith Crescent.

The area's most significant construction event of 1967 was the opening of a 12 storey residential building at 100 York Gate Boulevard. This was the first apartment building in the Jane-Finch area. It would take a decade for the area's skyline to be completed.[9] Westview Centennial Secondary School opened at 755 Oakdale Road with York-Finch General Hospital right across the road at 2111 Finch Avenue West.

The 17 storey Northgate and Southgate Towers were built at 2801 and 2775 Jane respectively in 1968. Yorkwoods Village was extended over to the south side of Grandravine Drive. Jane Junior High School (later renamed Brookview Middle School) was opened at 4505 Jane.

The Driftwood Towers (14 storeys) at 45 Driftwood Avenue, the Sandalwood Towers (15 storeys) just east of the Jane-Finch Mall at 1825 Finch Avenue West, and Newglen Towers (13 storeys) at 25 Stong Court all went up in 1969. So did the 13 storey Oakdale Terrace Apartments, built at 2600 Jane Street right across from a sprawling 4 storey low rise at 2770 Jane. Edgeley Apartments (12 storeys) opened at 35 Shoreham Drive on the east side of Jane, while St. Augustine Catholic School opened on the west side at 98 Shoreham Drive which was not yet extended over to Jane. The southwest corner of Jane-Finch was slowly developing, with houses being built on Blaney Crescent, Petiole Road, and Picaro Drive.

In 1970, the houses along Sheppard had been replaced by Fairway Place (20 storeys) at 2000 Sheppard Avenue West and Lafayette Apartments (14 storeys) at 2020 Sheppard Avenue West. Also reaching skyward were Grandravine Apartments (16 storeys) at 235 Grandravine Drive, the Labelle Apartments (13 storeys) at 2850 Jane Street and The Tobermory (12 storeys) at 35 Tobermory Drive. A few steps away from The Tobermory, the York Woods Public Library was officially opened by the North York Public Library Board at 1785 Finch Avenue West. Shoreham Public School opened at 31 Shoreham Drive, and Firgrove Public School opened at 270 Firgrove Crescent.

1971 saw the rise of Brownview Apartments (14 storeys) at 50 Driftwood Avenue, Driftwood Gardens (12 storeys) at 335 Driftwood Avenue, Driftwood Gardens (12 storeys) at 345 Driftwood Avenue, The Planter (12 storeys) at 2755 Jane Street, and Edgeley in the Village (12 storeys) at 4645 Jane Street. St. Francis de Sales Catholic School opened at 333 Firgrove Crescent. Shoreham Drive going east from Jane was now connected to York University. The university opened its Keele Campus in 1965, but it had only been accessible from Keele Street and Steeles Avenue West.

In 1972, Blackwood Square (13 storeys) went up at 310 Niska Road, along with the eponymous 16 storey building at 415 Driftwood Avenue and the 15 storey building at 2999 Jane Street (Jane Yewtree) just south of the Jane-Finch Mall.

1973 seemed especially busy, with the construction of 2900 Jane Street (13 storeys), Jane Milo (12 storeys) at 4400 Jane Street with Milo Park Tower (14 storeys) next door at 4500 Jane Street, the Tower Apartments (12 storeys) at 15 London Green Court, a 12 storey building at 5 Needle Firway, Antica House (14 storeys) at 5000 Jane Street, and the Antica Towers at 4001 Steeles Avenue West. The west side of Shoreham Drive now extended to Jane Street, with the Jane Shoreham Shopping Centre anchoring the northwest corner of the intersection. St. Charles Garnier Catholic School opened at 20 Stong Court as a collection of portables. The building was completed by the start of the 1975-1976 school year. The southwest corner saw the completion of the housing subdivision based around Firgrove Crescent.

There was a lot of concrete poured in 1974 with Elmpark Manor 1 (15 storeys) going up at 235 Gosford Boulevard and Elmpark Manor 2 at 4750 Jane Street, two 16 storey Cedarbury Towers built beside each other at 355 and 365 Grandravine Drive, two more buildings at 2940 Jane Street (13 storeys) and 2970 Jane Street, and Finch Tobermory, a 24 storey building at 15 Tobermory Drive.

No apartment buildings were opened in 1975, but the OHC development known as the Grassways (Firgrove Crescent) was completed by then. Two more buildings were added to the area in 1976. One was a 13 storey building at 320 Niska Road. The other was the first of the buildings which made up the Palisades, the tallest building in the area, the 33 storey structure at 10 San Romanoway. The Palisades would be completed in 1977 with two 18 storey buildings at 5 and 25 San Romanoway. The 13 storey Bristol House built at 10 Tobermory Drive rounded out the residential apartment highrises that were built in the area. The Driftwood Community Centre was built at 4401 Jane Street.

For the purposes of this article, the various highrises were the driving force behind the rapid population growth. That's not to say that the area's development ended in 1977. There would be other major additions to the Jane-Finch area, such as the Yorkgate Mall (1991) and the Oakdale Community Centre (350 Grandravine Drive, 1997). As mentioned earlier, the sale and subsequent development of the Northwoods Golf Course would see a new subdivision spring up in the northeast corner of Jane and Sheppard around 1980.

And there may yet be one more addition. One section of land has basically remained untouched after all these years. It fronts on Finch and lies between Yorkgate Boulevard and Norfinch Drive. At various times, there have been proposals to build highrises, but nothing has come of this. At least not yet. Watch that space.[10]

Notes

[1] Richardson, Christopher. (2008). Canada's Toughest Neighbourhood: Surveillance, Myth and Orientalism in Jane-Finch. St. Catharines: Brock University, Faculty of Humanities and Social Sciences.

[2] http://www.torontoneighbourhoods.net/neighbourhoods/north-york/elia

[3] http://www.yorku.ca/act/janefinch.html

[4] http://en.wikipedia.org/wiki/Jane_and_Finch

[5] http://preview.tinyurl.com/n6jdvfn (http://www1.toronto.ca/city_of_toronto/social_development_finance__administration/files/pdf/area_janefinch_full.pdf)

[6] List of Toronto Neighbourhoods: http://preview.tinyurl.com/kzkxa3r

[7] John Sakamoto, "How Jane-Finch was born," *Toronto Star*, November 30, 1986.

[8] The City of Toronto Archives has a few years worth of Aerial Photographs available online at: http://preview.tinyurl.com/lnv897v

[9] A lot of the details regarding the highrise buildings came from TOBuilt, "A Database of Buildings in Toronto, Canada" at: http://www.tobuilt.ca/

[10] If the Finch Light Rail Transit line is ever built, this lot will be used to house the rail cars.

Three Levels of Government

Jane-Finch On The Move has held community forums in the past. Political issues receive a lot of attention, along with calls to demand accountability from area politicians. In order to hold a politician accountable, one needs to know that politician's responsibilities. There are three main levels of government in Canadian politics, each with its own set of responsibilities. Here's a brief primer on the three levels and how they affect residents of the Jane-Finch area.

The Municipal Level

This level of government is based in a city, town, or district, otherwise known as municipalities. The City of Toronto is divided into 44 Wards. Each Ward is represented by a Councillor who is elected in a municipal election. These elections are currently held every four years. During municipal elections, voters also choose a mayor and a school board trustee (either public or separate, depending on which school system you direct your taxes). This has been the case since 1997, when the six municipalities that made up Metropolitan Toronto were combined. In our current system, the mayor only has one vote, so it's important to get the support of a majority of councillors to win votes.

The Jane-Finch area is divided between Wards 7, 8, and 9.

Ward 7 goes west to the Humber River, north to Steeles Avenue West (which is Toronto's city limit), and south to Highway 401. Its eastern boundaries are a bit more tricky. In the north, Ward 7 goes along Steeles Avenue West and turns south at Highway 400 to Finch Avenue West. The boundary then goes west to Jane Street (the heart of Jane-Finch). It then goes south down Jane Street to Highway 401.

Ward 8 shares Highway 400 as a boundary with Ward 7. Steeles Avenue West is the northern limit and goes east to Dufferin Street. The southern boundary goes along Grandravine Drive to Keele, south along Sheppard Avenue West, and east to Allen Road (Dufferin gets a name change south of Kennard Avenue). This means three quarters of the Jane-Finch intersection is in Ward 8.

Ward 9's western boundary is Jane Street. Its northern boundary is Ward 8's southern limits (see the above paragraph). Allen Road is the eastern limit, and the southern limit is Highway 401.

Responsibilities at the municipal level

It could be said that the municipal level is the one that affects residents most directly. It's about collecting garbage, taking the bus (or subway), getting an ambulance, or calling the police. It's about subsidized housing, Ontario Works, and the quality of our drinking water. Want to adopt a pet or complain about a neighbour's noisy animal? Need a permit for your business, your dog/cat, or a function at a local park or community centre? These are all municipal services, and this barely scratches the list.

To learn more, call 311, visit http://www.toronto.ca/, or contact your councillor.

The Provincial Level

Canada is divided into ten provinces and three territories. Each province has its own government. Ontario is divided into 107 ridings. During provincial elections, we vote for a Member of Provincial Parliament (MPP), who is usually associated with a political party. The party that wins the most seats takes power. The leader of the winning party becomes Premier. The party that finishes second is called the Opposition.

Jane-Finch is located in the riding of York West. This riding has Steeles Avenue West as its northern boundary, going east along the Humber River south to Highway 401. The boundary goes west to Jane Street, heading up north to Sheppard Avenue West, east to Black Creek, north along Grandravine Drive, east to Keele Street, and straight up north back to Steeles.

Responsibilities at the provincial level

The province is responsible for areas such as education, health care, some natural resources, and road regulations. You deal with the province for documents such as driver's license, health card, vehicle registration, and birth certificate. The local MPP can help with such things as Ontario Student Assistance Program (OSAP), workplace safety, and Ontario Disability Support Program (ODSP). Learn more online at http://www.ontario.ca/

The Federal Level

Canada has 308 electoral districts (or ridings), with 106 of them located within Ontario. This will change by the next federal election (2015), with the addition of another thirty ridings, with fifteen of those in Ontario. Federal elections are similar to their provincial counterparts. Voters in each riding vote for a Member of Parliament (MP), who usually belongs to a political party. The candidate who gets the most votes wins the seat. The party that gets the most seats overall gets to govern in the House of Parliament located in Ottawa. The leader of the winning party is Prime Minister. The party that finishes second is the Opposition.

At the time of writing, the boundaries of the federal riding of York West are the same as those of the provincial riding.

Responsibilities at the federal level

The federal government is responsible for such things as the post office, the banking system, and national defense. Some of the services handled by Ottawa include the Canada Pension Plan and Old Age Security, Employment Insurance, and Immigration. The federal government issues documents such as Social Insurance Number, visitor's visas, and money. Go here to learn more: http://www.parl.gc.ca/

Jane-Finch On The Move
Terms of Reference

Jane-Finch On The Move was formed in 2007 as a grassroots group with support from a number of local organizations. By 2012, members took on all responsibilities for running our group. During the spring of that year, JFOTM members created a Terms of Reference document that reflected the group's evolution. We present it here in case other groups need a starting point to create their own Terms.

Jane-Finch On The Move
Terms of Reference - Ratified August 10, 2012

Mission Statement:

Jane-Finch On The Move is a grassroots group that promotes community solidarity and harmony, and strives towards removing systemic barriers that many members in our community face through the participation of all members of our community. We value positive change with a demand for peace, social justice and economic security for all.

Overview

Group actions are governed by respect for members, and flexibility to meet the needs and requirements of members. All rules, requirements, objectives, and definitions can be modified in decisions made by majority vote.

Section 1: Membership

Membership is open to anyone with an attachment to the Jane-Finch community. "Attachment" can be defined as being a resident, past resident, employed in the area, studying in the area, and any other definition accepted by group members. To be considered "resident", one must live in the area bounded by Steeles Avenue West (north), Keele Street (east), Sheppard Avenue West (south), and Highway 400 (west).

There is a minimum age limit of fifteen years, and no maximum.

Membership process: a potential member must attend three meetings consecutively, unless there is good cause. A potential member can be nominated by any group member at a general meeting prior to the potential member being allowed to attend meetings. See "Section 3: Meetings." Potential members are not entitled to collect honorariums or TTC tokens. See "Section 3: Meetings." After three meetings, members will vote on awarding membership, with a simple majority being needed to pass the motion.

All Members must sign the JFOTM Membership Agreement Form. Signing the Membership Agreement Form is confirmation that the member understands all material contained within this "Terms of Reference" document, and is willing to abide by all the principals as set out in the Mission Statement as well as the adopted City of Toronto Declaration of a Non-Discrimination Policy.

Revocation of Membership: Memberships can be revoked by a majority vote. Grounds for immediate dismissal include physical harm to another member, blatant discrimination or hatred, bullying members, and libel or slander. An ex-member may ask to be reinstated, and members will vote to allow the member to state their case at a meeting. A majority vote is required for reinstatement.

Contact Information: Members' contact information is confidential between them and the Chair and Vice-Chair, who are the only two members authorized to contact the membership. Only the Chair can contact members via email, and all email addresses will be hidden.

Section 2: Membership Responsibilities

Members are expected to participate to the best of their abilities. Attending group meetings is a basic way to participate. Given that circumstances may not allow a member to attend meetings, they must find a way to remain in contact with the group. At a minimum, they must keep in contact with the Chair. This can be done by replying to email messages. As well, members can participate in group activities outside of meetings that better fit their circumstances.

Conflict of Interest: members have to declare any conflict of interest, real or perceived.

Disputes: If there is an issue with another member, the member should contact the Chair before taking any other action. If the issue is with the Chair, the member should contact the Vice-Chair.

Section 3: Meetings
In order to make decisions, a General Meeting must have quorum of fifty percent members plus one. Members will vote, with a majority needed to pass.

Only members are allowed to attend meetings, with the exception being potential members and members' children. All guests, including members of other organizations, must be cleared by members at a prior meeting. In the case of an emergency, the Chair will contact as many members as possible.

Meetings are governed by Robert's Rules Of Order.

Honorariums: Members who attend general meetings are entitled to receive an honorarium and TTC tokens. The amount is subject to the group's approval. See "Section 5: Financials."

The Chair has the right to end a meeting.

Section 4: Group Positions

At this time, there are only two positions. If other official positions are required, members can create them as required through a majority vote at a General Meeting. The new positions will be added to an updated Terms as soon as possible.

These positions are chosen in an election with written ballots. The process will be overseen by two members. Elections will be held every two years.

Chair

Responsibilities of the Chair:

- Keep order at meetings
- Ensure the following are done: meeting minutes, prepare required reports, prepare funding proposals, secure a meeting place, obtain child care (as required), keep copies of receipts (in keeping with our

Trustee Agreement), tracking sheets (for meetings and work sessions), safeguard TTC tokens and cash for honorariums

- All the above duties can be delegated by the Chair if required, but the ultimate responsibility for completing the above duties still lies with the Chair. (Note: none of these duties can be delegated to non-members without group consent)
- Signing authority on all documents
- Finances and spending. See "Financials"
- Maintaining dialogue with the Trustee and keeping members up to date as required

Removal of Chair: if members are not pleased with the Chair's performance, any member can raise a motion to remove the Chair. This motion will be voted upon at a meeting attended by at least ninety percent of membership. The Chair can not be present in the room during the vote, which requires a simple majority.

Vice-Chair
Responsibilities of the Vice-Chair:

- Contact members
- Fill in when Chair is absent or removed
- Secondary signing authority

Section 5: Financials

The Chair is the only member authorized to spend money on the group's behalf. However, all spending decisions must be voted upon at a General Meeting. The group can give a blanket approval; for example, giving the Chair discretion to buy supplies and refreshments as required, but the Chair must keep all receipts.

Closing Words

We've spoken, and now we're here to listen. Please send your comments to voicesmatter@jfotm.com

We want to publish reactions on our web site. Let's start dialogues between people, organizations, community leaders, and anyone else who has ideas, opinions, and stories to share. Our goal is for this book to be the start of something bigger.

If you'd like to order a copy of this book, go to our web site located at www.jfotm.com

Acknowledgements

Jane-Finch On The Move would like to thank the City of Toronto's Access, Equity and Human Rights (AEHR) grant program. These funds supported various JFOTM initiatives for the years 2007 to 2011, and played a vital role in our group's development. For more information about this program, visit http://preview.tinyurl.com/krmr8oz

We'd also like to acknowledge Freedonia (www.freedonia.ca), a foundation which gave us funds in 2008 and 2009.

Last but definitely not least, the Jane/Finch Family and Community Centre (http://www.janefinchcentre.org/) has played a vital role in the development of our group. To this day, the Centre supports Jane-Finch On The Move with space and resources.

About the back cover

The back cover photograph captures the mural located on the south wall of the apartment building at 4400 Jane Street. Funded by the City of Toronto's Graffiti Transformation Project, the mural was painted in 2005. Most of the work was done by youth attending various JFCFC programs under the supervision of a professional artist.

This mural has a particular significance for Jane-Finch On The Move members because we regularly meet in a room located on the other side of that wall.

Made in the USA
Charleston, SC
17 February 2015